Schizophrenia

OTHER BOOKS OF RELATED INTEREST

Schizophrenia

Scott Barbour, *Book Editor*

Daniel Leone, *President*
Bonnie Szumski, *Publisher*
Scott Barbour, *Managing Editor*

Contemporary Issues
Companion

Greenhaven Press, Inc., San Diego, CA

Every effort has been made to trace the owners of copyrighted material. The articles in this volume may have been edited for content, length, and/or reading level. The titles have been changed to enhance the editorial purpose. Those interested in locating the original source will find the complete citation on the first page of each article.

Library of Congress Cataloging-in-Publication Data

Schizophrenia / Scott Barbour, editor.
    p. cm. — (Contemporary issues companion)
    Includes bibliographical references and index.
    ISBN 0-7377-0636-8 (pbk. : alk. paper) —
    ISBN 0-7377-0637-6 (lib. : alk. paper)
    1. Schizophrenia. I. Barbour, Scott, 1963–   II. Series.

RC514 .S334152 2002
616.89'82—dc21
                                                2001033015
                                                    CIP

© 2002 by Greenhaven Press, Inc.
P.O. Box 289009, San Diego, CA 92198-9009

Printed in the U.S.A.

CONTENTS

FOREWORD

In the news, on the streets, and in neighborhoods, individuals are confronted with a variety of social problems. Such problems may affect people directly: A young woman may struggle with depression, suspect a friend of having bulimia, or watch a loved one battle cancer. And even the issues that do not directly affect her private life—such as religious cults, domestic violence, or legalized gambling—still impact the larger society in which she lives. Discovering and analyzing the complexities of issues that encompass communal and societal realms as well as the world of personal experience is a valuable educational goal in the modern world.

Effectively addressing social problems requires familiarity with a constantly changing stream of data. Becoming well informed about today's controversies is an intricate process that often involves reading myriad primary and secondary sources, analyzing political debates, weighing various experts' opinions—even listening to first-hand accounts of those directly affected by the issue. For students and general observers, this can be a daunting task because of the sheer volume of information available in books, periodicals, on the evening news, and on the Internet. Researching the consequences of legalized gambling, for example, might entail sifting through congressional testimony on gambling's societal effects, examining private studies on Indian gaming, perusing numerous websites devoted to Internet betting, and reading essays written by lottery winners as well as interviews with recovering compulsive gamblers. Obtaining valuable information can be time-consuming—since it often requires researchers to pore over numerous documents and commentaries before discovering a source relevant to their particular investigation.

Greenhaven's Contemporary Issues Companion series seeks to assist this process of research by providing readers with useful and pertinent information about today's complex issues. Each volume in this anthology series focuses on a topic of current interest, presenting informative and thought-provoking selections written from a wide variety of viewpoints. The readings selected by the editors include such diverse sources as personal accounts and case studies, pertinent factual and statistical articles, and relevant commentaries and overviews. This diversity of sources and views, found in every Contemporary Issues Companion, offers readers a broad perspective in one convenient volume.

In addition, each title in the Contemporary Issues Companion series is designed especially for young adults. The selections included in every volume are chosen for their accessibility and are expertly edited in consideration of both the reading and comprehension levels of the audience. The structure of the anthologies also enhances accessibility. An introductory essay places each issue in context and provides helpful facts such as historical background or current statistics and legislation that pertain to the topic. The chapters that follow organize the material and focus on specific aspects of the book's topic. Every essay is introduced by a brief summary of its main points and biographical information about the author. These summaries aid in comprehension and can also serve to direct readers to material of immediate interest and need. Finally, a comprehensive index allows readers to efficiently scan and locate content.

The Contemporary Issues Companion series is an ideal launching point for research on a particular topic. Each anthology in the series is composed of readings taken from an extensive gamut of resources, including periodicals, newspapers, books, government documents, the publications of private and public organizations, and Internet websites. In these volumes, readers will find factual support suitable for use in reports, debates, speeches, and research papers. The anthologies also facilitate further research, featuring a book and periodical bibliography and a list of organizations to contact for additional information.

A perfect resource for both students and the general reader, Greenhaven's Contemporary Issues Companion series is sure to be a valued source of current, readable information on social problems that interest young adults. It is the editors' hope that readers will find the Contemporary Issues Companion series useful as a starting point to formulate their own opinions about and answers to the complex issues of the present day.

INTRODUCTION

At the age of twenty-two, Maurizio Baldini was a successful law student residing in Vancouver, British Columbia. He maintained an active lifestyle, jogging five miles four times a week and enjoying various outdoor activities, including tennis and mountain climbing. One fall day in October 1976, he felt unwell; believing he was delirious from the flu, he stayed in bed. However, as Baldini explains, his symptoms got worse:

> I began to have delusions about the state of the world around me. Suddenly the noises made by cars and planes going by outside my house took on secret and deliberate meanings. I became convinced that I was involved in the start of a nuclear war and the only way for me to survive was to find the answer to a difficult riddle. . . . I fluctuated between wild delusions of grandeur to deep depressions about my future. I thought I would become the next prime minister of Canada and rule by divine right over a new world order for our citizens. I was also visited by demonic voices.

Instead of the flu, Baldini was experiencing the onset of schizophrenia, a severe mental illness that affects the sufferer's perceptions and thought processes.

Contrary to popular belief, people with schizophrenia do not have a "split personality." Rather, they are split off from reality as most people experience it. There are two types of symptoms of schizophrenia: positive and negative. Positive symptoms, so named because they are the most obvious and easily identifiable, include hallucinations, delusions, and disorganized thinking and behavior. Hallucinations are sensory perceptions (usually sounds or sights) that have no origin in reality. The most common hallucinations experienced by people with schizophrenia are voices, which are often threatening or intimidating. Delusions are false beliefs, such as Baldini's conviction that he was involved in the start of a nuclear war. Other positive symptoms include disorganized, incomprehensible speech and disorganized behavior, such as wearing multiple overcoats on a hot day.

Negative symptoms of schizophrenia derive their name from the sense that something has been taken away from the person experiencing them. These symptoms include lack of motivation, social withdrawal, and reduced emotional expressiveness. People with schizophrenia frequently do not have the motivation to complete even the most basic activities of daily living, such as bathing and cleaning their clothes. They also often have a "flat" look on their face, showing little or no emotion and avoiding eye contact with others.

Unfortunately, the experience of Maurizio Baldini is not uncommon. Schizophrenia affects approximately 1 percent of the population worldwide. According to the National Institute of Mental Health, a government agency that conducts research on mental illness, over 2 million Americans are affected by schizophrenia, at a cost of $32.5 billion annually. In terms of human costs, 10 percent of people with schizophrenia commit suicide, and a large proportion of those afflicted experience some degree of lifelong disability. Schizophrenia affects people of all races, cultures, and walks of life in about equal numbers. Men are at a slightly higher risk for the disorder than women. In addition, men generally experience the onset of illness in their late teens and early twenties, whereas women typically experience their first symptoms in their late twenties or early thirties. People with schizophrenia tend to be disproportionately poor, but studies indicate that they become poor as a result of the illness; poverty is not the cause of the disorder.

Although a great deal of research is being done into the causes of the disorder, schizophrenia remains, as psychologist William O. Faustman states, "one of the most misunderstood of all human afflictions." Most theories regarding the cause of schizophrenia focus on biological factors. Comparisons of the brains of people with and without schizophrenia reveal differences in structure and functioning. People with schizophrenia have larger ventricles (fluid-filled spaces at the center of the brain) as well as a smaller volume of gray matter. These findings suggest that schizophrenia may be the result of the brain's failure to develop properly. Other research has concentrated on the activity of brain chemicals—especially the neurotransmitters dopamine and glutamate—which has been found to differ in persons with schizophrenia.

Most researchers agree that there is a genetic component to the disorder. Individuals with a schizophrenic family member are at an increased risk for the disease; the closer the relationship, the greater the risk. If one identical twin has schizophrenia, the risk of the other twin having the disorder is 48 percent. In fraternal twins, the risk is 17 percent; for non-twin siblings, a 9 percent chance. A child of a person with schizophrenia runs a 13 percent risk of developing symptoms. This evidence leads many to conclude that genetics plays a major role in the disorder.

However, researchers caution, genes alone do not cause schizophrenia. If genes were the sole culprit, identical twins—who share 100 percent of their genetic information—would have a 100 percent chance of co-occurrence. Therefore, genes are believed to be merely part of the puzzle. The disease only manifests itself if a person with a genetic predisposition for the disorder encounters certain environmental stressors, many experts contend. In past decades, an unstable family environment was believed to be the crucial agent; however, this theory has largely been disproven. Nowadays, most experts favor the theory that certain biological triggers can interact with a genetic predisposition to cause schizophrenia. One predominate theory is that if a pregnant woman is infected with a flu virus at a crucial stage of fetal development, the virus will adversely affect the child, who will have an increased risk of displaying symptoms of schizophrenia during adolescence or early adulthood. Despite various theories and ongoing research, experts concede that the precise cause of the disorder still remains unknown.

Similarly, there is no known cure for schizophrenia, although the symptoms of the disorder can be controlled by means of antipsychotic medications. The first medications to control the positive symptoms of schizophrenia—most notably Thorazine, Haldol, and Prolixin—were developed in the 1950s. While these medications were effective at reducing hallucinations and delusions, they had unpleasant side effects, including sedation, dry mouth, and the risk of tardive dyskinesia—a disorder that produces involuntary, bizarre movements of the mouth, limbs, and hips. Newer medications, such as Zyprexa and Risperdal, have fewer side effects and appear to alleviate some of the negative symptoms of schizophrenia as well as the positive ones.

Along with medications, mental health professionals generally recommend non-medical types of treatment designed to enable people with schizophrenia to cope with their disorder. These treatments include therapy to assist persons with schizophrenia to manage their medication, resolve everyday problems and interpersonal conflicts, and obtain appropriate living and work situations. Persons with schizophrenia often live in supported residential programs, which vary according to need from highly structured settings with close supervision to apartment-like living with minimal oversight. They are often able to find employment by means of vocational services or psychosocial clubhouses, day programs that are usually run by and for people with severe mental illnesses. These programs also provide them with much-needed support from people who share their experience of struggling with troubling symptoms and social isolation.

In recent years, a new approach known as assertive community treatment (ACT) has become increasingly popular. ACT programs center around interdisciplinary teams of psychiatrists, social workers, nurses, and vocational rehabilitation specialists who assist mentally ill people in their homes and workplaces. Under this model, the treatment team ensures that each person has medication, appropriate housing, social support, employment, and other services. These programs have been shown to reduce rehospitalizations by keeping mentally ill individuals stable in the community.

Although there is no cure for schizophrenia, and many people with the disorder experience a lifelong struggle with symptoms, there is evidence that a large number do recover and experience dramatic improvements in their quality of life. For instance, researchers in Vermont who followed up on a group of patients with schizophrenia after thirty-two years found that 68 percent had no symptoms of schizophrenia; this number included many who were no longer taking any medications. These findings suggest that the common belief that schizophrenia is invariably a chronic and permanently disabling disease is inaccurate. As Daniel Fisher, a psychiatrist who recovered from schizophrenia, asserts, "People with schizophrenia . . . are capable of regaining significant roles in society and of running their own lives."

The selections presented in *Schizophrenia: Contemporary Issues Companion* provide insight into the lives of people with schizophrenia. The authors included in these chapters examine the possible causes of the disorder, describe the various treatments available to help its victims, investigate the social impact of the disease, and illustrate the emotional toll it exacts on individuals and their loved ones. In doing so, they dispel the myths and misconceptions surrounding schizophrenia and reveal that those who suffer from its symptoms are ordinary individuals who face daunting challenges as the result of their condition.

CHAPTER 1

THE NATURE OF SCHIZOPHRENIA

DEFINING SCHIZOPHRENIA

National Institute of Mental Health

In the following selection, the National Institute of Mental Health (NIMH), an agency of the U.S. government that conducts research on mental illness, examines the nature and symptoms of schizophrenia. According to NIMH, schizophrenia is a brain disease that causes sufferers to experience distorted perceptions of reality, hallucinations, and delusions. Other symptoms include social withdrawal, a decrease in emotional expressiveness, and apathy. Although the exact cause has not yet been determined, the disorder is most likely transmitted genetically and probably involves an imbalance in neurological chemicals due to an abnormal brain structure, NIMH reports.

Schizophrenia is a chronic, severe, and disabling brain disease. Approximately 1 percent of the population develops schizophrenia during their lifetime—more than 2 million Americans suffer from the illness in a given year. Although schizophrenia affects men and women with equal frequency, the disorder often appears earlier in men, usually in the late teens or early twenties, than in women, who are generally affected in the twenties to early thirties. People with schizophrenia often suffer terrifying symptoms such as hearing internal voices not heard by others, or believing that other people are reading their minds, controlling their thoughts, or plotting to harm them. These symptoms may leave them fearful and withdrawn. Their speech and behavior can be so disorganized that they may be incomprehensible or frightening to others. Available treatments can relieve many symptoms, but most people with schizophrenia continue to suffer some symptoms throughout their lives; it has been estimated that no more than one in five individuals recovers completely.

This is a time of hope for people with schizophrenia and their families. Research is gradually leading to new and safer medications and unraveling the complex causes of the disease. Scientists are using many approaches from the study of molecular genetics to the study of populations to learn about schizophrenia. Methods of imaging the brain's structure and function hold the promise of new insights into the disorder.

Excerpted from "Schizophrenia," by the National Institute of Mental Health, NIH Publication no. 99-3517, 1999. Article available at www.nimh.nih.gov/publicat. schizoph.cfm.

Schizophrenia as an Illness

Schizophrenia is found all over the world. The severity of the symptoms and long-lasting, chronic pattern of schizophrenia often cause a high degree of disability. Medications and other treatments for schizophrenia, when used regularly and as prescribed, can help reduce and control the distressing symptoms of the illness. However, some people are not greatly helped by available treatments or may prematurely discontinue treatment because of unpleasant side effects or other reasons. Even when treatment is effective, persisting consequences of the illness—lost opportunities, stigma, residual symptoms, and medication side effects—may be very troubling.

The first signs of schizophrenia often appear as confusing, or even shocking, changes in behavior. Coping with the symptoms of schizophrenia can be especially difficult for family members who remember how involved or vivacious a person was before they became ill. The sudden onset of severe psychotic symptoms is referred to as an "acute" phase of schizophrenia. "Psychosis," a common condition in schizophrenia, is a state of mental impairment marked by hallucinations, which are disturbances of sensory perception, and/or delusions, which are false yet strongly held personal beliefs that result from an inability to separate real from unreal experiences. Less obvious symptoms, such as social isolation or withdrawal, or unusual speech, thinking, or behavior, may precede, be seen along with, or follow the psychotic symptoms.

Some people have only one such psychotic episode; others have many episodes during a lifetime, but lead relatively normal lives during the interim periods. However, the individual with "chronic" schizophrenia, or a continuous or recurring pattern of illness, often does not fully recover normal functioning and typically requires long-term treatment, generally including medication, to control the symptoms.

Making a Diagnosis

It is important to rule out other illnesses, as sometimes people suffer severe mental symptoms or even psychosis due to undetected underlying medical conditions. For this reason, a medical history should be taken and a physical examination and laboratory tests should be done to rule out other possible causes of the symptoms before concluding that a person has schizophrenia. In addition, since commonly abused drugs may cause symptoms resembling schizophrenia, blood or urine samples from the person can be tested at hospitals or physicians' offices for the presence of these drugs.

At times, it is difficult to tell one mental disorder from another. For instance, some people with symptoms of schizophrenia exhibit prolonged extremes of elated or depressed mood, and it is important to determine whether such a patient has schizophrenia or actually has a manic-depressive (or bipolar) disorder or major depressive disorder.

Persons whose symptoms cannot be clearly categorized are sometimes diagnosed as having a "schizoaffective disorder."

Can children have schizophrenia? Children over the age of five can develop schizophrenia, but it is very rare before adolescence. Although some people who later develop schizophrenia may have seemed different from other children at an early age, the psychotic symptoms of schizophrenia—hallucinations and delusions—are extremely uncommon before adolescence.

The World of People with Schizophrenia

• *Distorted perceptions of reality.* People with schizophrenia may have perceptions of reality that are strikingly different from the reality seen and shared by others around them. Living in a world distorted by hallucinations and delusions, individuals with schizophrenia may feel frightened, anxious, and confused.

In part because of the unusual realities they experience, people with schizophrenia may behave very differently at various times. Sometimes they may seem distant, detached, or preoccupied and may even sit as rigidly as a stone, not moving for hours or uttering a sound. Other times they may move about constantly—always occupied, appearing wide-awake, vigilant, and alert.

• *Hallucinations and illusions.* Hallucinations and illusions are disturbances of perception that are common in people suffering from schizophrenia. Hallucinations are perceptions that occur without connection to an appropriate source. Although hallucinations can occur in any sensory form—auditory (sound), visual (sight), tactile (touch), gustatory (taste), and olfactory (smell)—hearing voices that other people do not hear is the most common type of hallucination in schizophrenia. Voices may describe the patient's activities, carry on a conversation, warn of impending dangers, or even issue orders to the individual. Illusions, on the other hand, occur when a sensory stimulus is present but is incorrectly interpreted by the individual.

• *Delusions.* Delusions are false personal beliefs that are not subject to reason or contradictory evidence and are not explained by a person's usual cultural concepts. Delusions may take on different themes. For example, patients suffering from paranoid-type symptoms—roughly one-third of people with schizophrenia—often have delusions of persecution, or false and irrational beliefs that they are being cheated, harassed, poisoned, or conspired against. These patients may believe that they, or a member of the family or someone close to them, are the focus of this persecution. In addition, delusions of grandeur, in which a person may believe he or she is a famous or important figure, may occur in schizophrenia. Sometimes the delusions experienced by people with schizophrenia are quite bizarre; for instance, believing that a neighbor is controlling their behavior with magnetic waves; that people on television are directing special messages to them; or that their thoughts are being broadcast aloud to others.

Thought and Expressiveness

• *Disordered thinking*. Schizophrenia often affects a person's ability to "think straight." Thoughts may come and go rapidly; the person may not be able to concentrate on one thought for very long and may be easily distracted, unable to focus attention.

People with schizophrenia may not be able to sort out what is relevant and what is not relevant to a situation. The person may be unable to connect thoughts into logical sequences, with thoughts becoming disorganized and fragmented. This lack of logical continuity of thought, termed "thought disorder," can make conversation very difficult and may contribute to social isolation. If people cannot make sense of what an individual is saying, they are likely to become uncomfortable and tend to leave that person alone.

• *Emotional expression*. People with schizophrenia often show "blunted" or "flat" affect. This refers to a severe reduction in emotional expressiveness. A person with schizophrenia may not show the signs of normal emotion, perhaps may speak in a monotonous voice, have diminished facial expressions, and appear extremely apathetic. The person may withdraw socially, avoiding contact with others; and when forced to interact, he or she may have nothing to say, reflecting "impoverished thought." Motivation can be greatly decreased, as can interest in or enjoyment of life. In some severe cases, a person can spend entire days doing nothing at all, even neglecting basic hygiene. These problems with emotional expression and motivation, which may be extremely troubling to family members and friends, are symptoms of schizophrenia—not character flaws or personal weaknesses.

• *Normal versus abnormal*. At times, normal individuals may feel, think, or act in ways that resemble schizophrenia. Normal people may sometimes be unable to "think straight." They may become extremely anxious, for example, when speaking in front of groups and may feel confused, be unable to pull their thoughts together, and forget what they had intended to say. This is not schizophrenia. At the same time, people with schizophrenia do not always act abnormally. Indeed, some people with the illness can appear completely normal and be perfectly responsible, even while they experience hallucinations or delusions. An individual's behavior may change over time, becoming bizarre if medication is stopped and returning closer to normal when receiving appropriate treatment.

Violence and Suicide

Are people with schizophrenia likely to be violent? News and entertainment media tend to link mental illness and criminal violence; however, studies indicate that except for those persons with a record of criminal violence *before becoming ill*, and those with substance abuse or alcohol problems, people with schizophrenia are not especially prone to violence. Most individuals with schizophrenia are not violent; more typically, they are withdrawn and prefer to be left alone. Most violent crimes are not committed by persons with schizophrenia, and most persons with schizophrenia do not commit violent crimes. Substance abuse significantly raises the rate of violence in people with schizophrenia but also in people who do not have any mental illness. People with paranoid and psychotic symptoms, which can become worse if medications are discontinued, may also be at higher risk for violent behavior. When violence does occur, it is most frequently targeted at family members and friends, and more often takes place at home.

What about suicide? Suicide is a serious danger in people who have schizophrenia. If an individual tries to commit suicide or threatens to do so, professional help should be sought immediately. People with schizophrenia have a higher rate of suicide than the general population. Approximately 10 percent of people with schizophrenia (especially younger adult males) commit suicide. Unfortunately, the prediction of suicide in people with schizophrenia can be especially difficult.

What Causes Schizophrenia?

There is no known single cause of schizophrenia. Many diseases, such as heart disease, result from an interplay of genetic, behavioral, and other factors; and this may be the case for schizophrenia as well. Scientists do not yet understand all of the factors necessary to produce schizophrenia, but all the tools of modern biomedical research are being used to search for genes, critical moments in brain development, and other factors that may lead to the illness.

Is schizophrenia inherited? It has long been known that schizophrenia runs in families. People who have a close relative with schizophrenia are more likely to develop the disorder than are people who have no relatives with the illness. For example, a monozygotic (identical) twin of a person with schizophrenia has the highest risk—40 to 50 percent—of developing the illness. A child whose parent has schizophrenia has about a 10 percent chance. By comparison, the risk of schizophrenia in the general population is about 1 percent.

Scientists are studying genetic factors in schizophrenia. It appears likely that multiple genes are involved in creating a predisposition to develop the disorder. In addition, factors such as prenatal difficulties like intrauterine starvation or viral infections, perinatal complications, and various nonspecific stressors, seem to influence the development of schizophrenia. However, it is not yet understood how the genetic predisposition is transmitted, and it cannot yet be accurately predicted whether a given person will or will not develop the disorder.

Several regions of the human genome are being investigated to identify genes that may confer susceptibility for schizophrenia. The strongest evidence to date leads to chromosomes 13 and 6 but remains unconfirmed. Identification of specific genes involved in the development of schizophrenia will provide important clues into what goes wrong in the brain to produce and sustain the illness and will guide the development of new and better treatments.

Schizophrenia and the Brain

Is schizophrenia associated with a chemical defect in the brain? Basic knowledge about brain chemistry and its link to schizophrenia is expanding rapidly. Neurotransmitters, substances that allow communication between nerve cells, have long been thought to be involved in the development of schizophrenia. It is likely, although not yet certain, that the disorder is associated with some imbalance of the complex, interrelated chemical systems of the brain, perhaps involving the neurotransmitters dopamine and glutamate. This area of research is promising.

Is schizophrenia caused by a physical abnormality in the brain? There have been dramatic advances in neuroimaging technology that permit scientists to study brain structure and function in living individuals. Many studies of people with schizophrenia have found abnormalities in brain structure (for example, enlargement of the fluid-filled cavities, called the ventricles, in the interior of the brain, and decreased size of certain brain regions) or function (for example, decreased metabolic activity in certain brain regions). It should be emphasized that these abnormalities are quite subtle and are not characteristic of *all* people with schizophrenia, nor do they occur *only* in individuals with this illness. Microscopic studies of brain tissue after death have also shown small changes in distribution or number of brain cells in people with schizophrenia. It appears that many (but probably not all) of these changes are present before an individual becomes ill, and schizophrenia may be, in part, a disorder in development of the brain.

Developmental neurobiologists funded by the National Institute of Mental Health (NIMH) have found that schizophrenia may be a developmental disorder resulting when neurons form inappropriate connections during fetal development. These errors may lie dormant until puberty, when changes in the brain that occur normally during this critical stage of maturation interact adversely with the faulty connections. This research has spurred efforts to identify prenatal factors that may have some bearing on the apparent developmental abnormality.

In other studies, investigators using brain-imaging techniques have found evidence of early biochemical changes that may precede the onset of disease symptoms, prompting examination of the neural circuits that are most likely to be involved in producing those symptoms. Meanwhile, scientists working at the molecular level are exploring the genetic basis for abnormalities in brain development and in the neurotransmitter systems regulating brain function.

TYPICAL FEATURES OF SCHIZOPHRENIA

Richard S.E. Keefe and Philip D. Harvey

Richard S.E. Keefe and Philip D. Harvey present several key characteristics of schizophrenia in the following selection, including some early signs of the disorder, the typical age at which it develops, and the varied prognoses for persons afflicted with the illness. Harvey is a professor of psychiatry at the Mount Sinai School of Medicine in New York. He and Keefe are coauthors of *Understanding Schizophrenia: A Guide to the New Research on Causes and Treatment*, from which this selection is excerpted.

One of the principal questions that anyone who knows someone who develops schizophrenia asks is "Could I have known somehow?" There has been a significant amount of research on the pre-illness characteristics of persons who develop schizophrenia. The results of those studies suggest that there is a great deal of diversity in the way people look before the illness manifests itself fully, just as there is afterward. In fact, it is very possible to think mistakenly that the early signs of the illness should have been noticed. One problem with a lot of this research is that it has often been based on recollections by others of what the person with schizophrenia was like many years earlier. There is a completely natural tendency for people to change their recollections of long-past behavior to fit the current pattern; thus, if a parent has three children and one develops schizophrenia, it is likely that he or she will see that child in hindsight as having been different all along.

In the research that is not handicapped by this problem of recollection, several findings have appeared consistently. Social withdrawal and having few friends are factors that are often found. Relative to other children in their classes in school, children who later develop schizophrenia have fewer activities and fewer friends. Male children who develop schizophrenia are often poorly adjusted in terms of dating and relationships with the opposite sex. In fact, having no social or sexual experience with the opposite sex is a common feature of individuals who develop schizophrenia.

Another feature that appears in studies is the tendency toward unpredictable aggression. This aggression is not necessarily serious or frequent, but it does appear to be unpredictable; significantly, it often occurs in conjunction with social withdrawal. In the general population most aggressive behavior that children engage in involves regular contact with peers, with aggression often being directed against a victimized child. Children who go on to develop schizophrenia, however, are often unpredictably aggressive; for example, such a child may sit in the corner, ignoring the other children, and then suddenly punch someone who is walking by for no apparent reason. However, not all children who grow up to develop schizophrenia act this way; many do not have any notable maladaptive behavior during childhood. In fact, many of the children who grow up to develop schizophrenia do not stand out at all. This feature, a tendency toward lacking individuality, or possibly being difficult to approach or get to know, is probably related to the social withdrawal described earlier.

Not Strange Children

One thing that appears to be clear is that children who go on to develop schizophrenia are not typically strange. If anything, the symptoms they show before they develop schizophrenia are like mild versions of the negative symptoms of reduced emotional expression and reduced capacity to experience pleasure. It is quite atypical to see children who have mild versions of the positive symptoms [e.g., hallucinations and delusions] of the disorder before they develop schizophrenia. In fact, children who manifest symptoms of autism or other developmental disorders appear very different in adulthood from adults with schizophrenia.

Experiencing mild forms of hallucinations or delusions is actually not common in children who go on to develop schizophrenia. Some young adults who begin to seem unusual or strange (in terms of their dress, their ways of expressing themselves, and their beliefs) may eventually go on to develop schizophrenia. These early signs, which are referred to as the *prodrome* of schizophrenia, may develop months or even years before the full-fledged symptoms of psychosis. However, these people may also be experiencing an illness related to schizophrenia that is referred to as *schizotypal personality disorder*. Furthermore, since adolescence and young adulthood are commonly characterized by transitory periods of unusual behaviors (some parents maintain that adolescence *is* a diagnosis!), it is difficult to distinguish between someone who will eventually develop schizophrenia and someone who will go on to live a healthy and productive life.

Difficult to Predict

Many people who develop symptoms of schizophrenia and are helped by medication are indistinguishable as children from individuals who develop no psychiatric illness. It appears to be those who have a form of schizophrenia with a particularly poor outcome who are most identifiable when they are younger. One feature that has been found to occur in children who develop schizophrenia as adults, or other related illnesses (such as schizotypal personality disorder), is a set of subtle problems in attention that often resembles a very mild learning disability. These children may not perform quite up to their potential in school, although school failure is actually a rarity. The majority of people with schizophrenia who do not achieve well in school are actually showing symptoms of schizophrenia while still in school and do not finish for this reason. Much like some adult schizophrenic patients, many children who develop schizophrenia have problems in concentration and attention. These deficits are not severe, such as those seen in attention deficit disorder, and are often not linked with severe problems in learning or with very low IQ scores. Some studies have found tendencies on the part of people who later develop schizophrenia to have lower IQs before the onset of the overt signs of the illness, but this finding does not appear in every study.

There have been no successful studies on prevention of the development of schizophrenia on the basis of early indicators. One of the problems is that the indicators do not do a very good job of predicting the development of schizophrenia. Many children who never develop schizophrenia or any other neurobiological disorder as adults have mild problems with attention or periods of social withdrawal and unpredictable aggression. In addition, as we have indicated, many persons who develop schizophrenia could not be distinguished as children on the basis of anything that we know about now. It appears that children who have all of these indicators—attentional impairments, aggression, and social withdrawal—are at the highest risk of developing schizophrenia or a related disorder when they grow up, but these behaviors are not currently viewed as accurate predictors of who will develop schizophrenia. The individuals who are easiest to identify before they develop the illness also have the worst outcome in terms of poor response to medication and risk for lengthy stays in the hospital. One of the major goals of current research in schizophrenia is to identify the exact patterns of behavior that are present in individuals who are about to develop schizophrenia. The identification of these patterns may contribute to the development of intervention programs, involving social services or medication, to prevent the disorder from developing. Studies of family members of schizophrenic patients are often oriented at identifying signs of impending illness; at the current stage of research, however, the accuracy of these predictors has not been established.

Age at Onset

The age at which the first symptoms of schizophrenia occur varies considerably, in part because there is no clearly accepted definition of

what the first symptoms are. While the first delusions and hallucinations are usually obvious to people with schizophrenia and those
around them, the more subtle symptoms that may precede them—
such as slight reductions in cognitive functioning, social withdrawal,
loss of interest in usual activities, and strange thinking or behaviors—
can go relatively unnoticed. This is especially true for adolescents,
since their behavior is often unstable and difficult phases are virtually
the norm. Thus, the definition of what constitutes onset of illness is
controversial. As a result, the exact age at the onset of schizophrenic
symptoms is impossible to determine in many instances.

Despite the lack of precision in this area of research, some general
conclusions can be made about the age of onset of schizophrenia. Figure 1 illustrates the estimated cumulative percentage of people who
develop schizophrenia at different ages. The average age at which
symptoms develop ranges from about 21 to 27. Development of
symptoms in childhood is rare; fewer than 1% of people with schizophrenia become ill before the age of 12. The period of greatest vulnerability to schizophrenia is during adolescence and young adulthood,
between the ages of 15 and 35. The development of schizophrenia
after age 45 is also rare: less than 10% of people experience their first
schizophrenic symptoms then.

There are several possible explanations for why the disorder develops during adolescence and young adulthood. Studies of brain development suggest that critical phases of brain maturation continue into

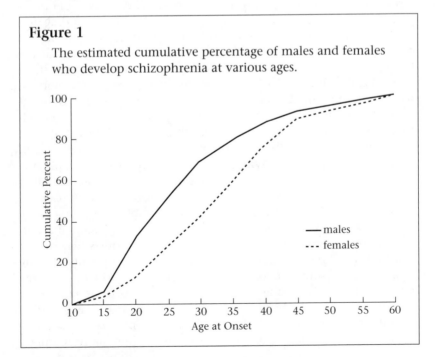

Figure 1

The estimated cumulative percentage of males and females
who develop schizophrenia at various ages.

late adolescence, and the final phases may be particularly important to ensure that a person is capable of navigating through the complex mental world of normal adulthood. The brain impairments that cause schizophrenia may render the brain unable to pass through these critical phases in adolescence. Alternatively, adolescence and young adulthood require the development of a relatively firm sense of identity and an ability to engage with other people. The brain impairments associated with schizophrenia can severely disable a young person's ability to develop these skills properly.

The Courses of Schizophrenia

One of the questions we often receive about the diagnosis of schizophrenia is "What can we expect? What will happen to this person?" The course of schizophrenia varies tremendously among different individuals. Because schizophrenia has such a dramatic impact on the life of the person with the illness, its course is heavily dependent upon many of the interacting influences in a person's life. Two people with the same symptoms at onset may have completely different outcomes. It is not really accurate to talk of the course of schizophrenia but of the courses, since the possibilities are so variable. The most common course of schizophrenia includes a gradual development of strange thinking, social withdrawal, and poor school or work performance, all of which lead to the realization by persons with schizophrenia or those around them that they are experiencing a *psychotic break,* that is, the first delusions, hallucinations, or severe communication problems. This initial psychosis, if treated swiftly and aggressively, can improve quickly. A general rule of thumb is that the length of time treatment, if successful, takes to have its full effect equals the length of time the person was experiencing symptoms prior to treatment. While a full remission of symptoms and a complete return to the same quality of life as before the onset of the illness is possible, it is less likely than a lifelong course of symptoms. The current definition of schizophrenia requires a 6-month period of illness, and most people do not fully recover from that long a period of symptoms. In fact, very short periods of symptoms similar to those of schizophrenia followed by complete remission are rare and suggest a diagnosis other than schizophrenia. People with these diagnoses, such as *schizophreniform disorder,* are much more likely to fare favorably in the long run.

It was initially believed that the presence of schizophrenia heralded a life of chronic institutionalization. Recent studies suggest that [because] psychologists treated and studied only people manifesting schizophrenia with a poor outcome, that is, those who required rehospitalization and long-term care, they developed the false belief that all people with schizophrenia fare poorly. Several recent studies, including one by the World Health Organization (WHO), have suggested that about half of all people with schizophrenia have only a single episode of psychosis, although lingering negative symptoms and subtle cognitive impairments may persist throughout their lifetime. A diagnosis of schizophrenia certainly does not mean that a person will be hospitalized for his or her whole life, an outcome that probably occurs in less than 5% of those with the disorder. . . .

Many people with schizophrenia require numerous hospitalizations throughout their lifetime. Rehospitalization, which usually includes treatment with medication and behavioral intervention, can have the effect of reducing positive symptoms, such as delusions and hallucinations, but the negative symptoms, such as lethargy and the loss of interest and pleasure, often remain. The neurochemical imbalances inherent in schizophrenia and the various stresses of life outside the hospital can lead to an increase in symptoms. These exacerbations of symptoms occur frequently in some people and often lead to rehospitalization. . . . People who respond well to medications often have the most hospital admissions, since those who cannot be helped by medication are more likely never to meet the requirements for hospital discharge and thus never need readmission.

About 5% of people with schizophrenia, those with the most severe forms of the illness, become completely dependent on others for their basic necessities and are never again able to live as independent adults. If they are not fortunate enough to have tremendous financial resources and extremely devoted caretakers or family members, they will likely remain in institutions or on the street for most of their lives. . . .

It is not clear why some people with schizophrenia fare well over time and others end up completely dependent on others. Surprisingly, the presence of seemingly dangerous and unusual symptoms, such as hallucinations and severe delusions, do not predict poor response to treatment and long-term institutionalization, and some of the symptoms that seem most benign, like a reduction in the normal intensity of emotional experiences and expression, are actually more foreboding predictors. Research on this issue suggests that a number of factors may predict a worse course of illness, including a history of schizophrenia in other family members, having few friends before the onset of the illness, particular abnormalities in the structure of the brain, and—somewhat counterintuitively—the *absence* of depression. Perhaps most importantly, people with schizophrenia who abuse street drugs, such as cocaine, amphetamines, heroin, and marijuana, during their illness are particularly susceptible to having a poor outcome. These kinds of drugs not only make the symptoms of schizophrenia worse but also interfere with the beneficial effects of the medications prescribed to help reduce symptoms. Although the research in this area is sparse, it is likely that a combination of factors, including differences in brain chemistry, is involved in causing some people with schizophrenia to fare so poorly over time while others improve with medication. Community differences may also be important: people with schizophrenia may get better support from others in rural areas than in large urban areas, where the unfortunate can more easily slip through the cracks of the impersonal support networks established by government agencies. No matter where a schizophrenic person lives, however, one fact is clear: the longer a person has symptoms, the longer the symptoms are likely to continue into the future.

Gender Differences

Males with schizophrenia and females with schizophrenia tend to differ in three significant ways: males tend to develop symptoms of schizophrenia an average of about 5 years earlier than females, they are less likely than females to marry and have children, and they tend to have a lower level of functioning than females in terms of social and school behavior patterns before the onset of schizophrenic symptoms. Gender differences in the course of schizophrenia may be related to the following general research findings: women are more likely than men to report psychological discomfort, more likely to take the medications they are prescribed, and more likely to improve following drug treatment. Since women with schizophrenia are less likely to be viewed as unmanageable or a danger to themselves or others, they are also less likely to be hospitalized involuntarily. In general, males with schizophrenia appear to have a more severe form of illness than females, but the magnitude of the gender differences may be due to an interaction between the symptoms of schizophrenia and the usual differences between men and women, rather than to any particularly severe defect in those men. Since men in general tend to be more aggressive, noncompliant, and independent than women, these attributes may be particularly poorly affected by the mental disintegration that results from schizophrenia. Research on the biological differences between males and females with schizophrenia has been inconclusive thus far, as has speculation regarding differential causes of illness in males and females. . . .

Geographical Distribution

All areas of the world and all cultures have some form of severe illness that appears similar to schizophrenia. Some of the details of the illness may differ in different cultures, as the content of thought of people in different cultures differs, but the general picture of symptoms is the same. People in even the most underdeveloped cultures have an awareness of the strange behaviors of some members of their society. Eskimo cultures in northwest Alaska and Yoruba cultures in rural tropical Nigeria, despite many dissimilarities with Western culture, were found by anthropologists to have words for hallucinations and delusions, as well as a label for an illness characterized by the symptoms of schizophrenia. Several of the residents of a community in tropical Nigeria answered questions about mental illness by pointing to a man who, without explanation, had removed himself from the rest of the society and begun living on an anthill outside the village. In addition, the people of this culture were able to distinguish between religious shamans, who "act out of their minds but are not crazy," and people with apparent illness, who "act out of their minds and are crazy."

The rate of schizophrenia appears similar in non-Western and Western cultures. However, there is some evidence that it is more prevalent in some geographical areas than in others. Recent studies suggest that there are two trends in the distribution of schizophrenia across the world: there appears to be more schizophrenia in the northern hemisphere than in the southern and, perhaps related to this, more schizophrenia as one moves away from the equator toward the poles of the earth. The causes of this geographical distribution of schizophrenia are not known. Some researchers have pointed to genetic differences among the people of different geographical regions whereas others have suggested that environmental differences between the regions are the causal factor.

Schizophrenia appears to have been present across the ages as well. The very earliest writings discovered include thinking that today would be considered delusional (of course, these ideas were not delusions, since they are consistent with cultural norms), but also found in these early writings are descriptions of people who had unusual mental experiences that were interpreted as painful for them to endure and difficult for the rest of their society to manage. Since early people interpreted much of their experience in terms of religious or mythological thought, the symptoms of schizophrenia were usually interpreted this way as well. Instead of believing their thoughts were being transmitted by satellites and hearing voices coming from microwave ovens, individuals with schizophrenia saw visions of dragons and heard the voices of the evil gods of their time.

Like many things, schizophrenia is more than the sum of its parts. If the parts of schizophrenia are its symptoms, the rest of the illness involves the consequences of the symptoms, including a variety of major life disruptions. Different persons with schizophrenia have different courses of illness and vary tremendously in terms of their occupational functioning and their risk for behaviors such as violence and suicide. In fact, many of the associated features of schizophrenia—occupational disability, homelessness, and self-destructive behavior—have as negative an impact on the lives of persons with schizophrenia as do the classic symptoms of the illness.

THE IMPACT OF SCHIZOPHRENIA ON FAMILY MEMBERS

Michael Ferriter

As Michael Ferriter describes in the following selection, the immediate family members of persons with schizophrenia often experience stresses, such as financial strain and overwhelming caretaking responsibilities, that can lead to resentment toward the ill relative. According to Ferriter, as family members deal with the diagnosis, they pass through various phases—from efforts to minimize the problem, to attempts to identify the cause of the disorder, to grieving "what might have been" had the family member not fallen ill. Ferriter is a research fellow at Rampton Hospital Authority, a forensic psychiatric hospital in North Nottinghamshire, England, and the author of *Schizophrenia and Parenting*, from which this selection is excerpted.

J.M. Atkinson lists several types of emotional burden found in families of people with Schizophrenia. She writes:

> Inevitably, relatives of chronic schizophrenic patients are worried about the present and the future, in terms of the patient's treatment and management. The past may also be of concern to them and provide an additional source of worry. Not infrequently there is a 'search after meaning' as relatives try to understand why this should have happened to their family. Many parents will feel that it is something they have or have not done that is at the root of the problem. They may search for anything in the ill child's upbringing that distinguishes him from his siblings, and will recall anything from traumas and illness, to real or imagined rejection by other family members as being of possible significance.

Reactions of guilt and blame would be likely if the family was being directly held to blame by mental health care professionals. . . .

Authors such as C. Creer and J. Wing have reported that parents of people with Schizophrenia often felt that professionals held them to blame for their child's illness: 'Many parents recalled some doctor or social worker who implied or stated unambiguously that it was their fault the patient was ill'. Creer and Wing also report anecdotes from families of responses from professionals that were prompt, sympathetic, appropriate and efficacious. The problem, as Creer and Wing found, was that the best sort of services, from the family's point of view, were not always available and evenly distributed.

The picture Creer and Wing paint of the plight of families of people with Schizophrenia at the time of their study (1975) was of a group of people who were sometimes helped and sometimes hindered by the responses of professionals, but who were, in the main, left to their own devices to work out their own solutions.

Sources of Distress

On the whole, the major sources of distress and disruption for the families were not violent and aggressive behaviour but more often the effects of negative symptoms of the disorder, such as frustration at the apathy or slowness of the sufferer. They shared the distress of their family member's social incapacity and were unsure whether to acquiesce with the sufferer's desire for social isolation or whether it would be therapeutically better to encourage or coerce the sufferer into social situations. Scant help or advice seemed available from the professionals.

Some positive symptoms were both common and distressing, particularly bouts of over-activity and distress caused by, and in response to, auditory hallucinations. Many families had worked out coping strategies such as advising their family member to pace up and down the garden rather than the road outside. Families said that unless one had lived under such circumstances, it was impossible to appreciate the strain and stress of it all. There was fear of rapid mood changes, unpredictable behaviour and the fate of the schizophrenic child when the parents died or were too old to cope.

Subjective and Objective Burden

E.H. Thompson and W. Doll usefully differentiate between objective and subjective burden to the family of having a mentally ill family member at home. Subjective burden was defined as the feelings engendered by the experience, objective burden as the disruption caused by having the member at home. In a survey of 125 relatives in Cleveland, Ohio, they found the following: In terms of objective burden, 38 per cent of the subjects reported a financial burden, 30 per cent role strains, 30 per cent disruption of everyday routines, 50 per cent required to supervise and 20 per cent problems with neighbours. In all, 26 per cent of subjects reported no objective burden items, 46 per reported two or more objective burden problems and 27 per cent three or more problems. In terms of subjective burden, 46 per cent reported feelings of embarrassment, 72 per cent feelings of overload, 42 per cent feelings of entrapment, 27 per cent moderate resentment, 13 per cent severe resentment, 21 per cent feelings of moderate exclusion and 6 per cent feelings of severe exclusion. In all, 23 per cent reported no subjective burden items, 62 per cent one or two items and 15 per cent three or more items.

Thomson and Doll found no demographic correlates of types of emotional burden and concluded that 'the emotional burdens of coping with a mentally ill kin appeared to be universally found in this sample, with no respect to differences in social classes, race, education, the age or sex of the relative or of the former patient'.

A similar lack of correlation was found in terms of objective burden with the one, obvious, exception that the lower the socio-economic group of the relative, the more likely they were to report the mentally ill family member as a financial burden.

Families Need Help

In a similar study, A.B. Hatfield had surveyed the burden to families of people with Schizophrenia in the Greater Washington area. Of the 89 usable questionnaires she received, she noted emotional burdens of stress, anxiety, resentment, grief and depression and the problems of causing hardship for siblings, threat to the parent's marriage, disruption of family social life, disruption of the personal life of family members and placing the burden on one member of the family. She concludes:

> The study found that the families of the mentally ill risk deterioration of their psychological and physical resources to the point that their personal efficiency may be reduced and the organisation and stability of their family life threatened. Humane considerations require that society take notice and create services to minimise this distress . . . People generally fear most what they do not understand. Therefore, the families of schizophrenic patients would be greatly helped by a knowledge of schizophrenia and practical techniques for managing patients with this disease. Also needed are professional relationships that include families as well as patients and in which family members are considered part of the treatment team and are assisted to understand the nature of schizophrenia and its prognosis and treatment. A recent study reported that care-givers who were asked what kind of help would most reduce their stress gave first priority to an understanding of schizophrenia and practical management techniques.

> They also expressed dismay that such help had been so persistently denied them by professionals to whom they had turned. A different type of professional may be needed in this area and literature of a non-technical nature should be widely distributed.

Siblings of People with Schizophrenia

The literature on the family and Schizophrenia tends to concentrate on parents of people with Schizophrenia but having a Schizophrenia sufferer in the family can have an impact on siblings.

N. Dearth, B.J. Labenski, M.E. Mott and L.M. Pellegrini, in their review of the experiences of members of the Families of the Mentally Ill Collective in the USA, look in some detail at the plight of brothers and sisters of sufferers. They found that the following reactions were typical.

Siblings may fear that they too may become mentally ill or that their own children might inherit the disorder; they may be the first member of the family to guess that something is wrong (particularly if they share a bedroom with the sufferer) and may meet with initial incredulity from their parents or suffer guilt because they did not make their fears known. Before or after family and professional realisation of the existence of the disorder, they may bear the brunt of their ill sibling's disruptive behaviour and this may affect their own education and social life. The behaviour of their schizophrenic sibling may lead to embarrassment and shame. Hospitalisation can be a point of shock as siblings are unlikely to be familiar with the ambience of the mental hospital and the impact of medication and this will compound the stress of visiting. In turn, siblings sometimes feel guilt at leaving their brother or sister in hospital—that they can walk away—and guilt that they can lead a normal and enjoyable life. They might also feel that their behaviour and comments are being scrutinised by mental health care professionals for evidence of mental illness.

Some siblings experience a sense of loss, akin to a sense of death, about their mentally ill brother or sister, a feeling that their sibling is irrevocably lost. They may also become prematurely aware of their mother and father's fallibility and vulnerability as their parents try to make sense of the family cataclysm. Indeed, the illness may generate disputes within the family. Finally, siblings of people with Schizophrenia frequently experience a premature sorrow and responsibility. This can lead to a psychological maturity and wider vision in advance of chronological years but it can also lead to resentment and be destructive.

Partners and Children

As Schizophrenia often becomes manifest before the time when one would expect the sufferer to form permanent relationships and have children—and the illness itself is associated with impaired social functioning and anhedonism [lack of interest in pleasurable activities]—people with Schizophrenia, on the whole, have a lower than average rate of spouses and established partners and children (leaving to one side the speculative argument that Schizophrenia may, in itself, be associated with lowered fertility). For these reasons, the literature on partners and children of people with Schizophrenia is not rich.

Schizophrenia may destroy a relationship. Through its combination of negative and positive symptoms, the person with Schizophrenia can be difficult to live with. The children of such relationships may suffer neglect or become the supportive adult in the family. They, like the siblings above, may fear inherited mental illness, feel resentment at premature responsibility and embarrassment at their parent's eccentric behaviour. The impoverishment that often is the result of the disorder will affect material standards in the home. . . .

The Evolution of the Family Response

K. Terkelsen attempts to map out the typical stages that the family might go through with their mentally ill member.

In the first phase, the family sees only minor symptoms, perhaps as minor variations in the subject's normal behaviour. Terkelsen argues that, as there is a dread of mental illness in society, there will be an inclination in the family to minimise such signs or hope that the subject will grow out of them. Even when family members do seek early and prompt assistance, it is not usually with any suspicion of a serious disorder.

The next phase is characterised by an event or events that disrupt the pattern of the family's adaptation to the subject's mental state. This can be a sudden escalation of deviant behaviour, an outside person bringing home the reality of the situation, or the more concerned family member seeking the help of a professional. The family may either seek help themselves or do what they can to make the subject change—to 'pull him/herself together'.

Terkelsen describes the third stage as stalemate, as the sufferer is not usually as advanced in realisation that something is profoundly wrong as the family. The family itself may be split as to the extent of the problem, indeed, mental health care professionals may themselves tend to minimise the problem or may concentrate on the family, now confused and anxious, as the seat of the problem. The family may well diverge, some to retreat from the problem, others to focus on the sufferer at the expense of other family members, while normal family problems and stresses get pushed to one side.

In the fourth stage, the family may still be experiencing anxiety but are not yet aware of the poor prognosis and outlook. This stage is characterised by various mechanisms for circumscribing the problem including: withdrawal, minimising the problem, denying the problem or defining it in terms of character problems of the sufferer, or recognising that the sufferer is ill but being hopeful that a cure will be forthcoming and the sufferer will revert to normal before long.

The Family Member as a Patient

Then, usually, an incident occurs. The sufferer is violent to others, attempts suicide etc., and the authorities now take cognisance of the sufferer who now becomes a patient. The meaning of mental illness for the family can no longer be ignored. At this point, the family or individual family members will embark on a search for the cause of the disorder. This search for a cause can take many forms. . . . There may be recriminations concerning the ill member's upbringing or the family may look to recent life events as aetiological [causative] factors. They may look at ancestry to detect supposed inherited insanity and, of course, this can be divisive as to whose side the taint of insanity comes from! Siblings and children may express anxiety, and issues of genetic counselling emerge. The family may consult scientific literature and, at this point, may be made aware that the world of psychiatry may not have many certainties to offer. The family may well split on aetiological lines.

Associated with the search for cause will be the search for cure or treatment and at this point the family may be exposed, for many for the first time, to the world of the hospital and the clinic. This world includes not just issues of medication but the whole panoply of issues: ward and hospital routines, mental health legislation, professional roles and boundaries, psychological based treatments, welfare rights and services in the community.

Where do the families gain this knowledge from? Frequently the staff seem too busy to do any more than answer direct questions, and though formal induction programmes and packs are becoming increasingly common for new patients to a hospital, clinic or other facility they are less common for patients' families.

Pessimism and Surrender

The next phase Terkelsen describes as the collapse of optimism, in which over weeks, then months, then years it becomes obvious that cure and reversion to the pre-morbid [pre-illness] state is unobtainable. Some benefits may be noticed such as control of positive symptoms by medication and the return of limited ability to lead a normal life, to maintain perhaps basic self care or sheltered work. All this may be characterised by remission and reoccurrence of the illness, of steps backward and forward. Some family members may see the patient as a total invalid and be over solicitous of his or her needs; other family members may be repelled by the patient and his or her behaviour and avoid contact. Any imbalance in the family, where individual family members may focus so much on the sufferer that other family members' needs go unmet, may also be a source of lasting resentment.

The penultimate phase Terkelsen calls 'surrendering the dream' and it is at this point that grief and a sense of loss of what might have been becomes important. In the case of Schizophrenia, the illness frequently manifests itself in early adulthood, and the family have memories of a normal childhood. Inevitably, there is a tendency to extrapolate as to what might have been, careers, families and so on, and the contrast between what is and what might have been is a poignant one. In this sense, the fluctuations in the disorder, the remissions and improvements, hinder rather than help in this process. A sudden improvement may offer tantalising hope of those dreams coming true and can lead to constant uncertainty. Conversely, professionals often complain that families react inappropriately or unenthusiastically to improvements in the sufferer's mental state. This may be explicable in terms of the family having seen the cycle of improvement and decline before. They will have a longer temporal perspective than that of the professional.

For the family, respite periods in residential care are highly desirable or the sufferer may be placed outside of the family home altogether and family contact managed at a tolerable level. But, as Terkelsen points out, the reality is that for many families compartmentalisation, the prerequisite for the well-being and normality of the individual and the family in the face of the catastrophic nature of the disorder, is incompatible with care at home.

CHAPTER 2

WHAT CAUSES SCHIZOPHRENIA?

Examining the Causes of Schizophrenia

William O. Faustman

William O. Faustman is a clinical and research psychologist at the Veterans Affairs Palo Alto Health Care System and a clinical associate professor in the department of psychiatry and behavioral sciences at the Stanford University School of Medicine. In the following selection, he presents the findings of research into the causes of schizophrenia, most of which point to a biological source for the illness. For example, Faustman writes, people with schizophrenia tend to have brains that differ in structure and chemical makeup from those without the disorder. In most cases, he concludes, healthy brain development is probably impeded by a combination of a genetic predisposition and obstetric or prenatal complications—setting the stage for the onset of symptoms of schizophrenia in adolescence or early adulthood.

Schizophrenia is one of the most misunderstood of all human afflictions. Most people would define the illness as some form of split personality, a "Dr. Jekyll and Mr. Hyde" disorder in which individuals show dramatic personality shifts. Even more tragically, schizophrenia is viewed by some people as a form of character weakness. . . .

Lay people often find the disorder frightening and impossible to comprehend. How could a young adult who was previously normal start to believe that aliens are inserting thoughts into his brain through a transmitter, or begin to have auditory hallucinations of voices that seem completely real? Throughout most of human history, people have turned to explanations based on spiritual possession and demons. To make matters even worse, schizophrenic individuals frequently "drift" to lower socioeconomic classes and must endure severe poverty and homelessness along with the stigma and suffering of a psychiatric illness. Until recently, the mentally ill have had few advocates to promote a proper understanding of the disorder. . . .

In the 1800s, Emil Kraepelin used the term *dementia praecox* to describe a disorder that differs little from the schizophrenia criteria found in modern-day diagnostic systems such as the *Diagnostic and*

Excerpted from "What Causes Schizophrenia," by William O. Faustman, in *Treating Schizophrenia*, edited by Sophia Vinogadov. Copyright © 1995 by Jossey-Bass, Inc. Reprinted with permission from Jossey-Bass, Inc., a subsidiary of John Wiley & Sons, Inc.

Statistical Manual of Mental Disorders IV. He employed the term *praecox* to emphasize that, unlike the dementia of old age, this disorder emerged early in life. Kraepelin considered the possibility that schizophrenia was based in "organic" or brain pathology, as did Eugen Bleuler, who coined the term *schizophrenia* in the early twentieth century. Though both of these early authors theorized about a "toxic" basis for schizophrenia, technologies of that day could not provide useful data about the biology of the illness.

Psychoanalytic theories regarding schizophrenia evolved over the years. These viewpoints suggested that disruptions in the mother-infant relationship and other developmental factors such as childhood psychological trauma could predispose an individual to schizophrenia. Furthermore, disturbed family relationships and communication styles were proposed as being common in the families of origin of schizophrenic individuals. Psychoanalysts believed that the accumulation of a disturbed sense of self, trauma, and difficulties in normal development and family patterns produced such anxiety that the individual had to break with reality.

It is interesting that these theories do model the observed process of schizophrenic individuals—a break with reality and the development of a separate state of inner reality—but they do not account for the accumulated weight of the biological findings we will examine in the following sections.

The Emergence of Modern Biological Theories

In the 1960s, scientists had begun to recognize the role of brain neurotransmitters, substances that serve as the vital link in the communication between brain nerve cells. Small amounts of neurotransmitters are released from one neuron (nerve cell in the brain) and stimulate the receptor found on an adjacent neuron; this is how neurons communicate with each other.

One of the earliest biological theories came about when researchers noticed structural similarities between some neurotransmitters and drugs such as lysergic acid diethylamide (LSD). Since LSD and similar drugs can produce significant perceptual changes, such as hallucinations and distortions of reality, some investigators postulated that subtle metabolic brain abnormalities in certain individuals allowed them literally to metabolize their own "psychedelic" LSD-like substance, thus producing schizophrenia. Though this hypothesis (called the transmethylation hypothesis) has logical appeal, there has been little direct evidence for it over the years.

Dopamine is a neurotransmitter that plays an important role in a variety of brain functions. Dopamine systems near the center of the brain, in a region called the basal ganglia, are vital for the control of fine motor coordination and movement. Degeneration of dopamine systems in this region causes Parkinson's disease, an illness in which individuals show muscle tremor and slowed movement. Other dopamine pathways are located in the limbic system, a brain area important in the regulation of emotion and memory. In addition, dopamine neurons are involved in the frontal cortex, a highly evolved brain region vital to the regulation of behavior, motivation, emotion, and planning.

All the drugs that reduce the core symptoms of schizophrenia—drugs such as chlorpromazine (Thorazine), haloperidol (Haldol), and risperidone (Risperdal)—have been shown to block dopamine receptors in the brain. In fact, the ability of antipsychotic medications to block dopamine receptors (specifically, dopamine type 2 receptors, one of several types of dopamine receptors) correlates strongly with the clinical potency of medications in the treatment of the core symptoms of schizophrenia. In other words, drugs like haloperidol (Haldol) that require only a very small dose to treat schizophrenia—generally 5–10 mg per day—have the strongest ability to block dopamine receptors, while drugs such as chlorpromazine (Thorazine) that require larger doses to treat patients (200 to 1000 mg per day) are less potent at blocking dopamine receptors.

This ability to block dopamine receptors clarifies one of the major and unfortunate side effects of these drugs: Parkinsonian or extrapyramidal side effects. These are muscle side effects that visibly resemble symptoms of Parkinson's disease and include slowness, tremor, or shakiness. Antipsychotic drugs produce these unwanted effects by blocking dopamine in the same midbrain dopamine systems that are related to Parkinson's disease. Fortunately, new medications such as clozapine (Clozaril) and risperidone (Risperdal) are able to treat schizophrenia with few if any of these side effects.

These and other data were used to develop the "dopamine theory of schizophrenia" during the 1970s, and research in more recent years has offered further support for dopamine mechanisms in certain aspects of schizophrenia. However, the results of neuroimaging and neuropathology studies demonstrate that the dopamine theory may be oversimplified, as schizophrenia appears to be far more than a single neurochemical disorder. Accordingly, it is best to think of these findings as supportive data for the importance of a neurotransmitter in the disease rather than a full explanation of all aspects of the pathology of the disorder. . . .

The technological advances of the past twenty years have allowed major strides in research into the biology of schizophrenia. Following is a brief review of the biological findings that may be related to the etiology or cause of schizophrenia.

The introduction of computerized tomography (CT) scanning in the 1970s allowed for the first high-quality imaging of the brain. Dozens of studies have used CT scanning to examine the differences between groups of schizophrenic individuals and subjects without psychiatric illness, called control subjects. These studies show that schizophrenic individuals as a group tend to have increases in the size of their ventricles—fluid-filled spaces that are found in the center of the brain—as well as increased fluid in the sulci, the spaces between the folds of the cerebral cortex.

An increase in brain fluid volume suggests many different possible abnormalities in brain development. For example, a genetic abnormality in schizophrenia could produce problems with early brain development resulting in less brain tissue and larger ventricles. Likewise, direct trauma (lack of oxygen, brain injuries) could also produce changes in the structure of the brain. These brain changes in schizophrenia are present at the onset of the illness (first hospitalization) and are therefore not likely a result of adverse effects of medications or institutionalization.

Magnetic resonance imaging (MRI) provides far more detailed structural brain images. An advantage of MRI over CT is that it allows for a clear division of the brain into fluid, gray matter (the bodies of neurons), and white matter (nerve cell connective tracts). Some recent studies have demonstrated that schizophrenic individuals show decreased gray matter volume. This finding suggests either that nerve cell bodies have failed to develop normally in certain brain regions or that they were eliminated or pruned away sometime during normal brain development.

The differences between schizophrenic individuals and control subjects that have been found in these studies are of *statistical* but not *diagnostic* significance. In other words, even though the neuroimaging studies of the two groups look different overall, there is overlap between groups: some schizophrenic individuals fall in the range of the controls; the reverse is also true.

Postmortem Neuropathology Studies

Another source for understanding brain pathology is from postmortem autopsy studies. Such research shows that individuals with schizophrenia have detectable differences in brain structures and cells when compared to controls. Many of these recent studies have focused on structural qualities of the hippocampus and associated regions. These brain areas are part of the limbic system and lie deep in the temporal lobe of the brain: they are vital as a "relay" area between neurons in the cortex and other regions, and they play an important role in the regulation of emotion, the perception of experience, and memory.

Several types of research findings differentiate these brain regions in schizophrenic patients from individuals without schizophrenia. The hippocampus may be smaller in schizophrenic individuals, and it appears to show abnormal cell orientation. Rather than showing cells with patterns of normal alignment, the hippocampal cells of schizophrenic individuals tend to lack proper orientation.

What could give rise to these abnormal findings in the hippocampus and associated brain regions? Abnormal brain cell orientation suggests a failure of the brain to organize itself properly. The organization of the cells of the cortex of the human brain takes place during important stages of development in the fetus. Accordingly, these neuropathological findings could be evidence that fetal brain maldevelopment is a factor in the genesis of schizophrenia. Both genetic and environmental factors influence the development of the fetal brain. . . .

Risk Factors for Schizophrenia

Research in the etiology or cause of schizophrenia is inherently difficult, especially since researchers now feel that the disorder has multiple etiologies. Some of the likely risk factors reviewed in the following section are genetic, obstetric birth complications, and prenatal viral exposure. Perhaps some schizophrenic individuals have a very heavy loading on a particular risk factor—such as a strong family history of schizophrenia—and the illness in such a patient is due largely to this single factor. In others the disorder may be caused by a subtle mixture of multiple risk factors that act together, such as exposure to a viral illness during fetal development plus a difficult birth with a lack of oxygen. Given this mixture of risk factors, we can see how research in this area is quite complicated.

It has long been observed that schizophrenia sometimes runs in families and overwhelming evidence now supports a role for genetic factors. However, the genetics of schizophrenia appear to be subtle and complex, interacting with environmental factors in the development of the illness. Even in families with a high rate of schizophrenia, most family members do *not* show the core symptoms of the illness such as hallucinations or severe delusions.

The genetic influences on schizophrenia are apparent in many ways. For example, family studies demonstrate that the closer in relation someone is to a person with schizophrenia, the greater the likelihood will be for that individual also to have schizophrenia. There is roughly a 10 percent chance that a person will have schizophrenia if he or she has a brother or sister with schizophrenia; this is about ten times the average in the general population. A child of two schizophrenic parents has approximately one chance in three of having the illness, or about thirty-three times the level in the general population. Though these observational family studies lend support for the genetics of schizophrenia, they are open to criticism since they do not control for environmental or psychological variables in the family, which could cause the disorder.

Twin studies have shown that the risk of schizophrenia in dizygotic (nonidentical) twins is the same as observed for siblings in family studies. However, there is approximately a 50 percent risk of a monozygotic (genetically identical) twin having schizophrenia if the other twin is affected with the illness. These findings are compelling since we can assume that identical and nonidentical twins experience a similar upbringing, but the results remain open to criticism about other environmental factors.

Adoption Studies

A series of brilliant studies performed in Denmark in the 1960s and 1970s helped to resolve some of the criticisms raised in family and twin studies. A team of investigators examined the rate of schizophrenia in over five hundred biological and adoptive relatives of adults who had been adopted as young children. Some of these adopted children had grown up to have schizophrenia while others did not. The researchers found that the biological relatives of individuals with schizophrenia had a higher rate of the disorder than did the adoptive relatives who had actually raised them. This finding is strong evidence for the genetics of the disorder rather than family environment since it was the *biological* and not the adoptive relatives who were more likely to have schizophrenia. Thus, genetic influences outweighed environmental or psychological variables in contributing to the incidence of schizophrenia in the adoptees.

Adoption studies have provided interesting observations about some of the relatives of schizophrenic individuals. A portion of family members of schizophrenic patients may share features of schizophrenia without demonstrating the full-blown characteristics of the disorder such as hallucinations or significant thinking disturbances. Some family members have features of oddness, eccentric personalities, or social withdrawal. These traits were used to develop the diagnostic criteria for what is known as schizotypal personality. Individuals with schizotypal personality traits show characteristics such as unusual perceptual experiences and magical thinking. Researchers believe that these features may represent an inherited trait of mild features of schizophrenia.

The relatives of schizophrenic patients tend to have higher rates of a range of psychotic disorders other than schizophrenia, including schizoaffective disorder and delusional disorder. Individuals with schizoaffective disorder show schizophrenic symptoms such as hallucinations, with mood disorder symptoms such as depression or mania. Delusional disorder patients have fixed psychotic beliefs—for example, that they are under observation by the Central Intelligence Agency and that their house is wired with transmitters—without the presence of other schizophrenic-like symptoms such as hallucinations. These findings suggest that the genetics of schizophrenia are also related to a range of other psychotic disorders.

Technologies developed in recent years allow for genetic linkage studies, in which sophisticated laboratory techniques permit scientists to test whether the distribution of schizophrenia in families is related to specific locations on various human chromosomes. Some initial findings of linkage to a location on chromosome 5 were reported, but unfortunately, other research groups have not been able to repeat this finding. Other studies have also been unable to find a consistent genetic link for schizophrenia.

Studies attempting to demonstrate genetic linkage for schizophrenia face numerous obstacles. Schizophrenia is far more difficult to diagnose in a reliable manner than medical conditions like cystic fibrosis or Huntington's disease, which have themselves required many years of research to determine their genetic linkage. Schizophrenia is relatively uncommon even in families who have a high rate of the disorder, and this low frequency of occurrence makes tying the disorder to a specific gene quite difficult. In addition, schizophrenia may be a genetically complex disorder, where multiple genes interact together to give rise to the illness. Another possible etiological basis of schizophrenia is in undocumented brain insults and injuries early in development. Thus, some individuals could develop schizophrenia with little or no genetic contribution, further confounding research studies directed at obtaining a genetic linkage.

In sum, there is compelling evidence that schizophrenia is to some degree a genetic disorder. However, genetics alone may not explain all or even some cases of the illness. Schizophrenia may be genetically quite complicated, and the identification of a specific schizophrenia gene or genes will be difficult.

Genetics helps to explain some facets of the etiology of schizophrenia. However, cases of schizophrenia are often sporadic, occurring in families in which there have been no individuals affected with psychiatric disorders for many generations. Growing evidence suggests that other, environmental factors may be a risk factor in the development of schizophrenia.

Obstetric Birth Complications

As noted previously, brain imaging studies in schizophrenia show evidence that the brain has failed to mature in a normal manner or has sustained a form of trauma or insult. Schizophrenic patients typically have no known personal history of head injuries that could produce such findings; however, obstetric and birth complications may be a risk factor for the later development of schizophrenia in young adulthood.

The types of complications encountered during pregnancy and delivery that are important for us to consider are quite diverse. Complications during pregnancy include serious physical injury to the mother or the use of medications that have warnings regarding their use in pregnant women. An extended labor or difficulties at delivery can result in oxygen deprivation to the baby. Some studies have found that obstetric complications are roughly twice as common in individuals who later develop schizophrenia than in a combined large sample of people with other psychiatric disorders. This work has noted that obstetric complications were significantly more common in schizophrenic patients who did not have a family history for schizophrenia than in those with such a family history.

Prenatal Viral Exposure

Exposure to influenza during the second trimester (the fourth through six months) of pregnancy may be a risk factor for the much later development of schizophrenia in young adulthood. The data for these studies have been derived from epidemiological records of northern European countries such as Finland, Denmark, and England where in the past fifty years there have been several influenza epidemics. During these epidemics a large percentage of the population fell ill for a brief period of time. Since many of these countries maintain excellent birth and psychiatric treatment records, researchers can examine the birth dates of individuals who in adulthood developed schizophrenia and attempt to find an association between increases in these births and influenza epidemics.

Several studies have noted a unique association between influenza epidemics and birth rates of schizophrenic individuals who would have been in the second trimester of fetal development at the time of their exposure to the epidemic. No associations have been found between influenza epidemics and schizophrenia rates for persons who would have been in the first or third trimester of fetal development at the time of the epidemic.

This association with the second trimester has unique implications in terms of brain development. During a portion of the second trimester, the human brain undergoes extensive organization and development. Brain cells migrate out from inner brain regions to form the layers of the cortex at the outer portions of the brain. We could hypothesize that exposure to a virus during these critical periods of brain development could have permanent effects on the cellular and general structure of the brain. However, we must remember that correlation is not causation. In other words, just because two things appear to be associated does not necessarily mean that one directly causes the other. Perhaps factors other than the viral exposure itself are creating the association. For example, when people become ill, they often take a variety of medications, and such treatments in pregnant women could influence fetal brain development and the link to later schizophrenia.

In addition to the rapid cell migration that occurs in the brain during the second trimester, this period is also the time in which the skin cells of the fingertips form the ridges that become fingerprints. The fingertip ridge counts of identical twins who were discordant for schizophrenia (one twin has schizophrenia, the other does not) were examined in recent research. Identical twins typically have extremely similar fingertip ridge counts; however, in this interesting research much greater differences were observed between the ridge counts in discordant twins than would be normally expected. These results have been interpreted as further evidence that subtle injury to the fetus during the second trimester may be important in the etiology of schizophrenia.

More Research Needed

Some data fail to support parental viral exposure as a risk factor for adult schizophrenia. For example, one study did not find any relationship between influenza epidemics and subsequent schizophrenia in several samples. More recent work has used a different approach to address the question of influenza and schizophrenia. While prior studies employed general population statistics (for example, influenza epidemics and general schizophrenia birth rates) to seek associations, they did not examine whether a *specific* individual with schizophrenia who was in the second trimester of fetal development during the epidemic actually had a mother who suffered from influenza. Recent research used data from a child development study in which detailed pregnancy histories had been obtained for all babies born in England, Scotland, and Wales during a week in 1958. Psychiatric records were then used to seek a relationship between an individual having schizophrenia in adulthood and also having a mother with an actual reported second trimester infection with influenza. No relationship was found between the documented second trimester influenza infection and schizophrenia in the individuals studied by the time they were twenty-seven years of age.

To summarize, some evidence supports a relationship between influenza epidemics and schizophrenia birth rates, though recent data suggest that further work on this question is needed. It may not be influenza alone that is a risk factor. For example, exposure to influenza may need to be combined with genetic vulnerability to produce an elevated risk for schizophrenia. Some studies that establish a relationship between viral epidemics and schizophrenia note that the findings account for only a small percentage—less than 10 percent—of schizophrenia cases.

Adolescent Brain Development

All the evidence we have examined suggests that events that may represent risk factors for schizophrenia occur early in life or even before birth. In addition, the genetic studies imply that some people are born with a gene (or genes) which puts them at risk for developing schizophrenia. Why, then, do the core symptoms of schizophrenia commonly manifest in late adolescence or early adulthood? Why don't they appear early in life?

These are some of the most interesting questions facing psychiatric researchers. In a pivotal paper, Irwin Feinberg proposed that the onset of schizophrenia may be related to maturational processes of the brain that do not occur until about the second decade of life. The human brain undergoes significant changes during the period from childhood to late adolescence, so an abnormality present at birth may not cause any problems until an individual is past childhood. For example, young children who suffer brain injuries to regions involved in speech can show a recovery of language function. However, if an adolescent or adult suffers an injury to exactly the same location there is often little or no chance of a significant recovery of function. This and other evidence suggest that important brain change or maturation takes place between childhood and adulthood that could determine whether an early brain abnormality causes a clinical syndrome.

There are also major changes in the pattern of sleep during adolescence, including a 50 percent reduction in some forms of sleep brain wave activity. This in turn may be related to the normal process of a reduction in some of the connections between brain cells that occurs during adolescence. Problems related to this normal "pruning" of brain cell connections could thus be related to the onset of schizophrenia in late adolescence or early adulthood.

This idea—that the process of normal human brain development in adolescence is important in the onset of schizophrenia—leads us to consider two hypotheses. One hypothesis is that an error in the programmed development of the brain is important in the expression of schizophrenia. Such an error in the brain's development could well have genetic origins. Thus the genetics of schizophrenia may in fact be related to the genetics of neurodevelopment. A second hypothesis is that there is an interaction between normal adolescent brain changes and preexisting factors, such as early brain injury, that then results in the onset of schizophrenia. The interaction between normal human brain development and schizophrenia risk factors will be an important topic of future investigations. . . .

A Complex Disorder

Research into the causes of schizophrenia is inherently difficult, for it appears to be a complex disorder with multiple factors that contribute to its etiology. Genetic factors certainly play a role in some cases, though the genetics of schizophrenia are probably quite complicated. For example, multiple genes may be responsible for the development of the illness. In addition, environmental insults such as obstetric complications and prenatal viral exposure may also play a role in the genesis of schizophrenia. These various factors may contribute solely to the presence of the condition in any given individual, or they may interact. Thus, genetic loading in one person with a strong family history of schizophrenia may be the major etiologic factor, while an interaction of genetic and environmental insults may cause the disorder in another person.

All the etiological factors for schizophrenia are likely to be genetically complicated and environmentally subtle and hard to detect, occurring many years before the onset of the illness. Further work is warranted on how these factors interact with normal brain development to produce the onset of schizophrenia in young adulthood. Given this long list of complexities, we can see why research progress in the etiology of schizophrenia requires great patience.

Neurological Changes During Adolescence May Trigger Schizophrenia

Elyse Tanouye

Recent brain research may explain why schizophrenia strikes during the late teens and early twenties, Elyse Tanouye relates in the following article. She explains that during adolescence, the human brain undergoes a sort of "spring-cleaning" in which particular circuits are disconnected and discarded in order to prepare the brain for the tasks of adulthood. In people who develop schizophrenia, researchers hypothesize, either the brain has too few connections to begin with or the process goes too far; in either case, essential neurological links are eliminated, resulting in disorganized thoughts, hallucinations, and other symptoms of schizophrenia. Tanouye is a staff reporter for the *Wall Street Journal* newspaper.

One of the great unsolved mysteries of schizophrenia is its method of attack—unexpected, swift and almost always during late adolescence and young adulthood. Understanding why it attacks in this way may provide a key to deciphering the causes of the disease and someday, scientists hope, a cure.

A growing number of brain researchers now believe schizophrenia's hallmark—the sudden onset of psychotic episodes at the end of a victim's second decade—can be explained by massive neural changes taking place in the human brain as people enter early adulthood.

Scientists believe during these years the normal brain embarks upon an intense biological form of spring cleaning, disconnecting and discarding many little-used circuits, or synapses. Scientists believe the process is a natural pruning of brain-cell connections that are essential for handling the explosive growth of information in a person's formative years. The pruning helps make the brain more efficient and flexible for handling the changing mental needs of adulthood.

Researchers including Thomas McGlashan, head of the Yale Psychiatric Institute of New Haven, Conn., suspect that schizophrenia patients also lose many vital neural connections during this cleanup process. Among the possible explanations: Their brains are overly aggressive pruners, or they have fewer of the critical nerve links to begin with, which then are destroyed during the cleanout.

A Window of Opportunity

Now, scientists hope to curtail some of the loss of nerve links in patients identified in schizophrenia's early, or "prodromal," stage. By administering new antipsychotic drugs, the researchers hope to diminish the intensity of the storm of cell trimming and the damage that results in the disease. If Dr. McGlashan's experiments and others are successful, they could provide significant evidence to back the pruning theory of how the disease arises and how to block it.

Dr. McGlashan suspects that for a person in the disease's prodromal phase, the window for intervention is short—about two years before onset and two years after. "My thought is we have a limited opportunity" to intervene and preserve crucial brain cell networks, Dr. McGlashan says. After early adulthood, when pruning ebbs, patients may even be able to stop taking the antipsychotic drugs.

The prodromal-pruning theory may shed light on several other possible explanations surfacing these days as scientists plumb the causes of schizophrenia. Some believe the disease is triggered by excessive emotional stress in youngsters whose genetics make them especially vulnerable to the illness.

Others think normal pruning exposes a different underlying vulnerability: Perhaps a viral infection or another event during fetal development damages the brain, leaving it vulnerable to schizophrenia later in life, when the abundance of neurons from childhood no longer masks and compensates for the damage. "Psychotic symptoms are the end result of a process" that begins much earlier, says Jeffrey A. Lieberman, vice chairman for research and scientific affairs and a psychiatry professor at the University of North Carolina medical school in Chapel Hill.

A Change of Focus

Scientists have come a long way in their understanding of schizophrenia in the past two decades. Back in the early 1970s, when Dr. McGlashan was trained as a psychoanalyst, much of psychiatry focused on conflict and environmental stress as the cause of the disease. After practicing psychoanalysis for a number of years, Dr. McGlashan conducted a landmark study in the early 1980s of severely ill schizophrenic patients, who underwent treatment including psychoanalysis with little benefit.

That led him to focus on neurological explanations, and after joining Yale in 1990, he began focusing on schizophrenic brains during the earliest phases of the disease. In recent years, he was riveted by evidence that the sooner patients are treated after their first episode, the faster and more completely they recover and the fewer relapses they experience.

He helped launch a study in Norway and Denmark to see if a massive public-education media campaign about schizophrenia's early signs—difficulty concentrating, sleeplessness, suspiciousness—can get patients into treatment earlier. The results were dramatic: Instead of waiting an average of two years to seek treatment, first-time schizophrenia patients sought treatment only six months after the onset of psychotic symptoms. Dr. McGlashan and his colleagues are now studying these patients to verify that earlier treatment makes a difference.

It had occurred to Dr. McGlashan that even before the first schizophrenic episode, damage to the brain is already done and irreversible. An even better strategy, he thought, would be to prevent the neurological damage in the first place. Could antipsychotic drugs do that? The drugs appear to prevent relapse, he says, and if you think of the first episode as a relapse, then perhaps that can be prevented too. He designed a clinical trial, now taking place at the Yale Psychiatric Institute, to find out.

Patrick D. McGorry, a psychiatry professor at the University of Melbourne, in Australia, whose work in at-risk patients sparked much of the current interest in schizophrenia, thinks hormones released during stressful experiences may somehow affect the brain structure. He notes that animal studies show the same sequence. Adolescence and young adulthood are a time of high stress, as people develop relationships, move away from home and wrestle with their own identities. For that reason, talk therapy teaching at-risk people how to manage stress is important, he says.

Stress also may play a role in the fetal-virus theory. Dr. Lieberman, of the University of North Carolina, thinks that as these vulnerable people try to cope with going off to college and other major life transitions, more demands are placed on damaged neurons. He notes that the age of onset for the disease tends to be later in China and India, suggesting that these societies' demands aren't as great, or that their family support systems are stronger, during this period.

Dysfunctional Families Cause Schizophrenia

John Modrow

John Modrow, who experienced a schizophrenic episode as a teenager, is the author of *How to Become a Schizophrenic: The Case Against Biological Psychiatry*, from which the following selection is excerpted. Modrow rejects the currently popular theory that schizophrenia is a genetically transmitted, biologically based brain disease. Instead, he believes it is a response to unhealthy family relationships. Children in "schizophrenogenic families" are manipulated and emotionally strained by their parents' neediness, hostilities, and mental instability, Modrow contends. Their schizophrenic behavior, he argues, is the inevitable outcome of growing up in such an unhealthy environment.

Before I explain how people become schizophrenic it is only reasonable to ask: what is schizophrenia? Although innumerable theories exist that purport to explain the exact nature and origin of schizophrenia, schizophrenics, as people, can be viewed only in one of two ways: as basically similar to other people, or as basically different. The dominant view is that of the medical model, which asserts that schizophrenics are so different from other people that they must be studied and treated as if they were alien creatures; that the actions, beliefs, and experiences of schizophrenics are not manifestations of their humanity, but of a mysterious and terrifying disease; and that schizophrenics constitute a genetically distinct group of inferior and dangerous people who must be kept locked up and/or drugged to the point of stupor. The other—or heretical—view emphasizes the fact that the so-called "symptoms" of schizophrenia are mental traits common to all mankind which have been exaggerated in schizophrenics due to environmental stress; that if any person were to be put through the same types of stress that schizophrenics have undergone, that person would become a schizophrenic; that "schizophrenics," as such, do not exist, but rather they are human beings who have undergone terrifying, heartbreaking, and damaging experiences, usually over a long period of time, and as a consequence are emotionally disturbed—often to the point of incapacitation. I have adopted this latter view.

Disturbed Family Relationships

My view that schizophrenia is not a disease is shared by an increasing number of authors including Thomas Szasz, R.D. Laing and Aaron Esterson, Theodore Sarbin and James C. Mancuso, and many others. Moreover, despite a recent and deplorable trend, psychiatry itself has been gradually abandoning the medical model throughout most of the twentieth century. For instance, in the early years of this century, Sigmund Freud discovered psychological causes for phenomena once believed to be caused by disease. Furthermore, as far back as 1906, Adolf Meyer, the founder of modern American psychiatry, argued that schizophrenia was not a disease entity but merely the result of a deterioration of habits. Building upon the foundations laid by Freud and Meyer, Harry Stack Sullivan was able to construct a coherent and convincing theory of schizophrenia as a grave disorder in living, traceable to specific traumatic incidents in the individual's life. A logical extension of Sullivan's approach are the studies that have been done on the families of schizophrenics by researchers at Palo Alto, California, Harvard University, Yale University, the National Institute of Mental Health, and in Great Britain, France, West Germany, and Finland. These researchers have demonstrated that schizophrenia is not a disease entity which can be localized within a single individual but is instead merely a part of a larger pattern of disturbed family relationships. Some examples are as follows:

The Abbot Family. Mr. and Mrs. Abbot appeared to be very sensible and ordinary people. Their daughter, Maya, had been diagnosed as a paranoid schizophrenic with delusions of reference [belief that external events pertain to oneself]. Maya's major clinical symptom—her "ideas of influence"—consisted in her belief that she influenced other people and was influenced in turn in ways she could neither understand nor control. It took over a year of investigation to find out that her parents were, in fact, influencing Maya in a very strange way. Mr. and Mrs. Abbot would regularly conduct "telepathy experiments" on Maya without her knowledge. This they would do by using agreed upon nonverbal signals to communicate with each other in Maya's presence in order to see if Maya would be able to pick this up. It was their belief that Maya possessed special powers.

The Abbots are very typical of the parents of schizophrenic children. On one hand, they are extremely intrusive and are disinclined to permit Maya to have any autonomy whatsoever. On the other, they are totally impervious to Maya's needs, perceptions, and feelings. They interpret Maya's wish for autonomy and her bitter resentment at its being thwarted as merely a symptom of her "illness."

The Ferris Family. Roger Ferris has been diagnosed as schizophrenic. In his family, his parents mutually manipulate each other in order to maintain a facade of optimism and harmonious amiability. Discussion of emotionally sensitive topics in his family is strictly taboo. When either of his parents would discuss such a subject, the other parent would remain silent for days or even weeks on end. One of Roger's main symptoms is his long periods of silence which deeply worry his parents. Nevertheless, Roger is the only member of his family who would openly discuss such topics as sex. His parents wish Roger would keep silent on this subject.

That Roger was able to obtain a job as a salesman while he was still severely disturbed was viewed by both his parents as a miraculous sign of his sudden recovery. Though Roger selected the job himself, Mr. Ferris, in a private agreement with the employer, had promised to pay part of Roger's salary on the condition that he be hired. Roger, however, was left with the impression he had gained that job through his own effort. Mr. Ferris had also agreed to secretly follow Roger on his rounds in case he should need help. One of Roger's "delusions" was his belief that he was being watched.

Mrs. Ferris' manner in relating to Roger as evidenced in her body language and tone of voice was clearly sexually provocative. Roger's other delusion concerns his sexual seduction of older women.

Nobility

The Dolfuss Family. Emil Dolfuss, a 26-year-old schizophrenic man, had been returned from the Orient by consular authorities where he had been living out his religious delusions of saving the world. When he arrived at the psychiatric institute, he was formally dressed, ostentatious in his bearing, and very correct and grandiloquent in his speech. He expected everyone around him to obey his commands. While at the institute, his behavior gradually deteriorated, and he soon discarded his formal attire and went about dressed in his shorts.

He became catatonic. While in this state, his behavior consisted largely of rituals borrowed from various Eastern religions. Emil would hoard food in his room. He would also periodically gorge himself on meat then go on a strictly vegetarian diet. Emil worshipped light as something sacred and was terrified of darkness. At times Emil would kneel and pray before his sister, Adele, whom he believed was a goddess. Sometimes Emil thought he too was a god.

Emil Dolfuss came from a very interesting family whose style of life was suggestive of European nobility. All members of this household had to be formally dressed as they sat down to eat dinner together. Mr. Dolfuss was a wealthy manufacturer and inventor who spent most of his time when he was home in his bedroom studying Eastern religion and philosophy while dressed only in his underwear. Mr. Dolfuss believed he was a reincarnation of the Buddha. From his studies, Mr. Dolfuss conceived a bizarre religious cult which was shared by his entire family, including his domestic servant. One ritual of Mr. Dolfuss' religion was the ceremonial lighting of candles. Before this ritual, Mr. Dolfuss would deliver a long speech concerning the holiness of light. Mrs. Dolfuss believed Mr. Dolfuss was a great man, and that her sole purpose in life should be to serve him. She was also a food faddist. The nursemaid worshipped Mr. Dolfuss as a demigod. She treated Emil as if he were a prince and would alternate between spoiling and harshly disciplining him. She often slept with him.

These examples clearly show that schizophrenia is not a disease but merely a reaction to and expression of a disturbed family environment. . . .

Handicapped Parents

Since most parents of schizophrenics are well-meaning people who have been handicapped by their own upbringing, it is a gross injustice, as well as an oversimplification, to hold them responsible for causing their children to become schizophrenic. According to a number of investigators including R.D. Scott and P.L. Ashworth, schizophrenia must be viewed as the culmination of a series of progressively worsening personality disorders [maladaptive patterns of behavior, feeling, or thought] spanning three or four generations.

In their profoundly illuminating paper, "The Shadow of the Ancestor: A Historical Factor in the Transmission of Schizophrenia," Scott and Ashworth report several cases in which a parent has perceived the patient in terms of his or her experience with a mad relative. In some cases this parent viewed the patient as a virtual reincarnation of the mad relative destined for the same fate. Due to his or her experience with, and involvement in, a relative's madness, this parent has a secret fear of going mad. Prior to viewing the patient in terms of the mad relative, some parents admitted "looking for it" both in themselves and in their children before centering their attention exclusively upon the patient.

When these parents project their own fear of going insane onto the patient, three things happen. First, these parents no longer fear going insane themselves since the patient has become the carrier of this fear. Second, the parents then proceed to view and treat this child as if he or she were either insane or in the process of going insane. Third, this kind of treatment creates a self-fulfilling prophecy in which the parent's fear produces first anxiety, then psychotic panic in the child.

I find Scott and Ashworth's paper extremely significant since it suggests that schizophrenia is actually transmitted through the *belief* that madness is inherited rather than by heredity itself. However, I think these authors have overlooked two things. First, it is not necessary for a parent to have had a mad relative in order to fear going insane. This parent could be unstable for a number of reasons. For instance, a mother could undergo a postpartum psychotic episode and as a result acquire a lifelong fear of madness which she then projects onto her child. Second, this same mother may then view her child as a virtual reincarnation of a mad relative *of her spouse.* This more effectively distances her from the onus of insanity than if she were to view this child in terms of one of her own relatives. Furthermore, this maneuver could be a covert way of calling into question the sanity of her own husband and thereby castrating him as a man. I suspect this is a common pattern in families which Theodore Lidz has described as "schismatic."

Schizophrenogenic Families

The acknowledged pioneer in the family studies of schizophrenia is Theodore Lidz, now professor emeritus at Yale University, whose studies concerning schizophrenia have earned him four major scientific awards. Very early in his career Dr. Lidz extensively studied patients whose mental disturbances were due to brain lesions, metabolic disorders, and toxic conditions. Dr. Lidz soon came to the conclusion that his schizophrenic patients were in an entirely different category from the former patients in that they suffered no loss of memory, orientation, or intellectual potential.

The core of Dr. Lidz's investigation centers around seventeen families in which at least one member was schizophrenic. No group of families has ever undergone such a prolonged and intensive scrutiny for any purpose as have those families. Over a period of years, Dr. Lidz and his associates were able to compile such a mass of intimate and minute detail on each and every member of those families as to be the envy of any novelist. Although the number of these families is relatively small, hundreds of other families were also studied in a less intensive way by Lidz and his coworkers at the Yale Psychiatric Institute. These families all had such grave deficiencies and distortions as to be frankly "schizophrenogenic" in nature.

"Schismatic" and "Skewed"

Two predominant patterns characterize such schizophrenogenic families, patterns which Lidz terms the "schismatic" and the "skewed." According to Lidz, the schismatic family is marked by open marital discord, one in which

> . . . both spouses were caught up in their own personality difficulties, which were aggravated to the point of desperation by the marital relationship. . . . Neither gained support of emotional need from the other. . . . Each spouse pursues his needs or objectives, largely ignoring the needs of the other, infuriating the partner and increasing ill-will and suspiciousness. A particularly malignant feature of these marriages is the chronic "undercutting" of the worth of one partner to the children by the other. The tendency to compete for the children's loyalty and affection is prominent; at times to gain a substitute to replace the affection missing from the spouse, but at times perhaps simply to hurt or spite the marital partner.

Commonly, the child of such divisive families is caught in a bind because she finds that trying to please either parent provokes rebuff and rejection by the other. . . . In her attempt to salvage the parents' marriage and retain two parents, a child may accept the role of the family scapegoat . . . and behave in ways that seem to be the cause of the parental strife, masking their incompatibility, but at the cost of failing to invest her own developmental needs.

Lidz describes the skewed family as follows:

In the skewed family the focus of attention is apt to fall upon the mother who is termed "schizophrenogenic," a mother who is impervious to the needs of other family members as separate individuals and is extremely intrusive into her son's life. Yet, the very poor model the father provides the son and his inability to counter the mother's aberrant ways in rearing the children are also critical. Although the mother has serious difficulties in being close and maternal to her son when an infant, she soon becomes overprotective, unable to feel that the child can even exist without her constant concern and supervision. She does not differentiate her own anxieties, needs, and feelings from those of the child. The mother seeks completion through her son, and . . . wishes to have him live out the life she feels has been closed to her.

Mother's Ambitions

As an example of such a schizophrenogenic mother, Lidz tells of a very domineering woman author who at an interview would answer questions specifically addressed to her husband and would scarcely let him get in a word of his own. She was a woman with the fixed idea that her daughter was a literary genius who would some day be world famous. However, her daughter's real needs, personality, and aspirations were a matter of complete and total indifference to her. For this mother, her daughter merely existed to fulfill her own frustrated literary ambitions. She told Dr. Lidz she wished her daughter would become a great novelist and follow in the footsteps of her idol, Virginia Woolf. Upon hearing this Dr. Lidz warily commented, "But Virginia Woolf had psychotic episodes and committed suicide." Without hesitation the mother replied, "It would be worth it."

A few weeks after that interview Dr. Lidz visited that woman's daughter in the hospital while he was making his rounds. He noticed several novels by Virginia Woolf in the patient's room and asked her about them. She replied in a lifeless voice, "Mother sent them—she has a thing about Virginia Woolf." As the months passed, the patient spoke of her despair over her own literary ineptness, of her resentment at having to live out her mother's ambitions, and of her desire for a marriage in which she could help her husband assert himself. After she had recovered from her psychosis her mother took her home. There, while living in her mother's home, she relapsed and committed suicide.

Egocentric Parents

In all the families investigated by Dr. Lidz, either one or both parents were so egocentric as to be unable to differentiate their own needs and feelings from those of their child. In skewed families, one parent—usually, but not always, the mother—seeks completion through her child and is incapable of viewing him as anything but an extension of herself. Instead of learning to master events or to recognize his own feelings or needs, the child's energies and developing capabilities go principally into supporting his mother's precarious emotional balance, and into bringing meaning and fulfillment to her life. Thus, the emerging individuality is stymied by his subservience to his mother's needs; he comes to view the world almost exclusively through his mother's eyes, unable to clearly distinguish his own feelings and needs from those of his mother.

In schismatic families there is constant discord because both parents are markedly egocentric and treat each other, as well as their children, as mere functions of their own needs. The child is often caught up in the conflict, trying to unite the parents and sometimes succeeding only at the cost of becoming a scapegoat on which the parents can hang their own inadequacies, thus concealing their own fundamental incompatibility. In this case, too, the child's development as an individual is stunted and sacrificed to save his parents. Because of their egocentricities, the parents can usually maintain their emotional equilibrium by projecting their own inadequacies onto the child. But the child's situation is far graver. Whereas the parents can maintain their stability by distorting reality in accordance with their own needs, the child, in order to feel wanted by the parents, must deny or repress his own feelings and needs and distort reality in accordance with his parents' needs. Thus the child's orientation is parent-centered more than it is egocentric. . . .

Often people who have been labeled "schizophrenic" are viewed as a genetically distinct subspecies of infrahumanity, or at least as horrendously defective persons. But their defect has its origins in their love for their parents, a love so deep that they are led to sacrifice their needs, their individuality, and ultimately their sanity for the sake of their parents. The children who become schizophrenic are always the ones who are closest to their parents. By contrast, so-called "invulnerable" children, i.e. children who come from clearly schizophrenogenic homes who yet evince superior adjustment, keep their physical and emotional distance from their parents.

Schizophrenia Is Not a Brain Disease

Thomas Szasz

Thomas Szasz is a professor of psychiatry emeritus at the State University of New York in Syracuse. He has written numerous books challenging the concept of mental illness. Szasz insists that people are labeled "schizophrenic" not because they have an identifiable disease of the brain, but because society judges their behavior to be "insane." For instance, Szasz contends that auditory hallucinations—the primary symptom of schizophrenia—are simply acts of self-conversation. Although everyone engages in such self-conversation, according to Szasz, only people who talk to themselves in ways that are socially unacceptable—such as audibly and in public—are deemed to have schizophrenia.

Although the "mind" is not a biological entity or scientific concept, "it" is now regularly studied by biologists, neurophilosophers, neuroscientists, and psychiatrists, many of whom ignore the actual uses of the term and, instead, treat the mind as if it were the brain, or a function of the brain, or as if the words "mind" and "brain" were synonyms. To anyone who speaks English fluently, this claim must seem extremely odd. Nevertheless, there is no shortage of prominent persons who make precisely that claim. "The mind is the brain," states Daniel C. Dennett, professor of philosophy at Tufts University. "Brain and mind are one," writes Alan J. Hobson, professor of psychiatry at Harvard University. In his book, *The Rediscovery of the Mind*, John R. Searle, professor of philosophy at the University of California at Berkeley, coins a new English compound noun, "mind/brain," attributes "biologically basic intrinsic intentionality" to it, and claims that "meaning" is "grounded in" it. This cannot be right. Meaning is grounded in culture, memory, and language, not in an imaginary mind/brain.

In order to evaluate properly the merits of studies based on such claims and premises, we must not lose sight of the fact that the word "mind" is a part of our everyday vocabulary and that we use it most often, with the most far-reaching practical consequences, in psychiatry, law, and ordinary discourse. . . .

Excerpted from "Mind, Brain, and the Problem of Responsibility," by Thomas Szasz, *Society,* May/June 2000. Reprinted with permission from Transaction Publishers.

"Brain" vs. "Mind"

The meaning of the word "brain" (in English and other Western languages) and the object it names are clear and uncontroversial. The same cannot be said about the meaning of the word "mind." Until the seventeenth century, the word "mind" was used only as a verb: "to mind" meant to heed, which implied agency, intention, and will. Once "mind" became a noun, it was expected to refer to an object. Was that object a thing, like the brain, or an abstraction, like the soul? Anatomists and neurosurgeons never mistake the brain for the mind and never call it "mind." Why are most contemporary philosophers and psychiatrists so eager to treat the terms as synonyms?

Pragmatically, we infer the meaning of words from their uses. Clearly, when we talk about an individual's mind, we are talking about him as a person, but when we talk about a person's brain (or other organs), we are not. Specifically, we use the word "mind" in lieu of the word "person" when we attribute legal or psychiatric non-responsibility or incompetence to him.

Organs, like the heart or the liver, can be defined by their functions; persons cannot. We rightly regard assigning a specific function to men or women and defining them by that function as the worst kind of political dehumanization. Disobedience is no less human nor less biologically "normal" than obedience. If we were to identify persons by a distinguishing function, that function would be existential-moral, not biological-medical; it would be the capacity and the duty to make choices and assume responsibility for them, a function we often attribute to the mind. These observations support the suggestion of George Herbert Mead that, if we wish to understand the mind, we must look to its connections with the self and society, rather than to its connections with the brain.

Actually, when we use the word "mind" in law or psychiatry, it stands for a reified-hypothesized "organ" that we treat as if it were the seat of responsibility. Let us not forget, or deny, that psychiatry is far more closely related to law than to medicine. In every advanced society, psychiatrists regularly make legally consequential pronouncements regarding the "competence" and "criminal responsibility" of individuals, resulting, respectively, in their being deprived of liberty or excused of crimes. These legal-psychiatric acts are older and more permanent in their character than the seemingly medical acts of diagnosing and treating mental disorders.

Self-Conversation Is Normal

The mind is dependent on language, as respiration is dependent on the lung. Minding, like breathing, is an activity, a doing. Doing what? Talking to oneself. Speech, the basic form of language, is oral and aural. Language as visual action—as writing and reading—is a later, far more complex, cultural and personal achievement. The linguistic building block we use to construct the mind is self-conversation. Self-conversation is the ability to have a conversation with oneself, the self acting both as speaker and listener, the "I" and the "me" speaking and listening, as one to another. When we talk to ourselves while asleep, we are dreaming. (Because inner speech is disinhibited during sleep, in our dreams we "say" and "see" things involuntarily.) When we talk to ourselves while awake—in ways permitted in our society—we are thinking or praying. And when we talk to ourselves while awake—in ways prohibited in our society—we are (said to be hallucinating and hence) crazy.

It seems to me self-evident that if a person is hallucinating—that is, if he claims to be "hearing voices" when no one is speaking to him—he is "hearing" his own inner voice. Who else's could he be hearing? In 1993, neurologists using neuroimaging studies showed conclusively that in the brain of the hallucinating person, Broca's area, controlling speech, not Wernicke's, controlling hearing, is activated.

People intuitively recognize that thinking is self-conversation and that speaking and listening to oneself are ordinary, normal acts. Children talk to their dolls and must learn to talk to themselves inaudibly. When cultural critic Harold Bloom tells a reporter that "The utility of literature is to teach us not how to talk to others, but how to talk to ourselves," we have no difficulty understanding what Bloom means. However, our cultural conventions limit our acceptance and understanding of self-conversation to certain contexts, especially humor, literature, and religion. "I like to talk to myself," quips comedian Jackie Mason, "because I like to deal with a better class of people."

The contemporary cultural rejection of the ordinariness of self-conversation and its psychiatric categorization as "hallucination" is reminiscent of the earlier cultural rejection of the ordinariness of erotic self-stimulation and its psychiatric categorization as "self-abuse" leading to "masturbatory insanity." We believe that hallucination is a manifestation of a severe mental/brain disease. For more than two hundred years—until mid-century—people believed that masturbation caused severe mental/brain disease. How convenient it is to forget!

To be accepted as sane (normal), the individual must acknowledge his self-conversation as his own (thinking) and must learn to talk to himself silently, in private. Talking to oneself audibly, in public (for example, as do "schizophrenics"), is better explained by attributing it to a dearth of sympathetic listeners or a preference for one's own company, than to brain dysfunction, albeit it may be present as well (for example, in senile persons who talk to themselves aloud).

What distinguishes hallucination or crazy self-conversation from its normal variant is what psychiatrists call "projection." I call it rejection of responsibility for one's own thoughts, for one's own identity, for who one is. The person said to be hallucinating disavows his thoughts and attributes them to "voices" originating outside of himself. We may say that a telephone directory is "telling" us that the number for Hotel X is such and such, but we do not claim that we receive that information through our ears, much less that we don't want to hear it. In contrast, prophets and some so-called psychotic persons claim that God is speaking to them or that they "hear voices" and insist that the messages are wholly external to them. If such a self-conversationalist attributes his voice to God, and if the authorities and people accept his claim as true, then they hail him as a prophet. If, however, he makes the same attribution and the authorities and people reject his claim as false, then they declare him to be a false messiah and ostracize him, if he lives in a religious culture, or, if he lives in a "rationalist" culture, they declare him to be mad and lock him up in an insane asylum. As I wrote some time ago: "If you talk to God, you are praying; if God talks to you, you have schizophrenia." In short, prayer is autologue validated by religion, whereas hallucination is autologue invalidated by psychiatry. A hallucinated perception implies a realistic perception from which it deviates. There can be no "hallucination" without "reality," and no "reality" without a (properly functioning) "mind."

Hallucinating, that is, talking to oneself—as though talking to another person—is a voluntary act. This does not mean that deciding to have one thought rather than another is like deciding whether to wear one tie or another. Nor does it mean that we cannot have unwanted thoughts, that is, inner voices—like Lady Macbeth's—reminding us of what we should not have done.

Like much of our behavior, our self-conversation or thinking is on automatic pilot. In that metaphorical sense, we may call it "unwilled." When an artist or scientist has a seemingly unintended (good) idea, we say he is "inspired" and call him a "genius." When an unhappy, unemployed person has an unintended (bad) thought, we say he "hears voices" and call him "mentally ill" (and attribute his "hallucination" to brain disease). To me at least, it seems very unlikely that the brain can distinguish between two acts that are similar in all important respects except with respect to the value we attach to each.

The paradigmatic act of self-conversation is our conscience, the inner judge that holds us responsible for what we do. The word "responsible" comes from the Latin respondere, which means to respond, hence its synonym, "answerable." Although we often say that a person "has" responsibility, that locution is misleading. A physician can examine a person's body to determine whether his kidney function is diminished or absent, because of renal disease; but he cannot examine a person's mind to determine whether "its" responsibility is diminished or annulled, because of mental disease—although that is precisely what the psychiatrist claims to be able to do and society accepts that he is able to do.

The language we use to speak about behavior largely determines our position on the issue of responsibility. The discourse of minding implies responsibility. The discourse of brain function does not. The law recognizes disease of the mind, but not disease of the brain, as a ground for civil commitment or as an excuse for crime. The proposition that "brain is mind" is not a fact or even a scientific hypothesis, as its supporters claim; instead, it is a rhetorical ruse concealing our unceasing struggle to control persons by controlling the vocabulary.

Insanity as an Excuse

In short, insanity is not simply a property of the Other or his brain; rather, it is an attribution the self creates for the Other, to protect himself from having to hold the Other responsible for certain misdeeds and to justify treating the Other with coercive paternalism, as if he were an infant or pet.

Not surprisingly, modern society's experts make frequent use of two tactics exploiting the conceptual dependence of moral agency on mindedness. One is attributing incompetence to the Other albeit he is, in fact, competent and wants to be so treated; the result is that we harm him under the guise of helping him. The other is treating the Other as a victim when, in fact, he is an agent, a victimizer of himself or others; the result is that we excuse him of responsibility for his self-victimization or the victimization of others.

Because the term "mind" is so richly evocative of what we mean by a person's self and his responsibility for his actions, it is impossible to speak or write about the connections between brain and mind in a moral vacuum—that is, without considering the impact of our views on psychiatry as one of modern society's most important instruments of social control. Although we may prefer to look the other way, the psychiatrist's two paradigmatic professional activities—depriving innocent persons of liberty (called "civil commitment"), and excusing guilty persons of crime (called the "insanity defense")—will not go away. As long as these practices prevail, the most common and most important uses of the term "mind" are its uses in psychiatry. And as long as that remains the case, we must acknowledge that our analysis of the brain-mind relationship will validate or invalidate, support or oppose the legitimacy and "rationality" of psychiatric coercions and excuses.

CHAPTER 3

TREATING SCHIZOPHRENIA

TREATMENTS FOR SCHIZOPHRENIA: AN OVERVIEW

National Institute of Mental Health

The National Institute of Mental Health (NIMH) is an agency of the U.S. government that conducts research on mental illness. In the following article, the institute surveys the various treatments available for people with schizophrenia. While no cure for schizophrenia exists, NIMH reports that the latest drugs, called atypical antipsychotics, are effective in treating some of the symptoms of the disorder, especially hallucinations and delusions. NIMH also describes the non-medical treatments, including social skills training, vocational counseling, psychotherapy, and family education, which help persons with schizophrenia live among the general population and enjoy an improved quality of life.

Since schizophrenia may not be a single condition and its causes are not yet known, current treatment methods are based on both clinical research and experience. These approaches are chosen on the basis of their ability to reduce the symptoms of schizophrenia and to lessen the chances that symptoms will return.

What About Medications?

Antipsychotic medications have been available since the mid-1950s. They have greatly improved the outlook for individual patients. These medications reduce the psychotic symptoms of schizophrenia and usually allow the patient to function more effectively and appropriately. Antipsychotic drugs are the best treatment now available, but they do not "cure" schizophrenia or ensure that there will be no further psychotic episodes. The choice and dosage of medication can be made only by a qualified physician who is well trained in the medical treatment of mental disorders. The dosage of medication is individualized for each patient, since people may vary a great deal in the amount of drug needed to reduce symptoms without producing troublesome side effects.

The large majority of people with schizophrenia show substantial improvement when treated with antipsychotic drugs. Some

Excerpted from "Schizophrenia," by the National Institute of Mental Health, NIH Publication no. 99-3517, 1999. Article available at www.nimh.nih.gov/publicat. schizoph.cfm.

patients, however, are not helped very much by the medications and a few do not seem to need them. It is difficult to predict which patients will fall into these two groups and to distinguish them from the large majority of patients who *do* benefit from treatment with antipsychotic drugs.

A number of new antipsychotic drugs (the so-called "atypical antipsychotics") have been introduced since 1990. The first of these, clozapine (Clozaril®), has been shown to be more effective than other antipsychotics, although the possibility of severe side effects—in particular, a condition called agranulocytosis (loss of the white blood cells that fight infection)—requires that patients be monitored with blood tests every one or two weeks. Even newer antipsychotic drugs, such as risperidone (Risperdal®) and olanzapine (Zyprexa®), are safer than the older drugs or clozapine, and they also may be better tolerated. They may or may not treat the illness as well as clozapine, however. Several additional antipsychotics are currently under development.

Antipsychotic drugs are often very effective in treating certain symptoms of schizophrenia, particularly hallucinations and delusions; unfortunately, the drugs may not be as helpful with other symptoms, such as reduced motivation and emotional expressiveness. Indeed, the older antipsychotics (which also went by the name of "neuroleptics"), medicines like haloperidol (Haldol®) or chlorpromazine (Thorazine®), may even produce side effects that resemble the more difficult-to-treat symptoms. Often, lowering the dose or switching to a different medicine may reduce these side effects; the newer medicines, including olanzapine (Zyprexa®), quetiapine (Seroquel®), and risperidone (Risperdal®), appear less likely to have this problem. Sometimes when people with schizophrenia become depressed, other symptoms can appear to worsen. The symptoms may improve with the addition of an antidepressant medication.

Worries and Misconceptions About Medications

Patients and families sometimes become worried about the antipsychotic medications used to treat schizophrenia. In addition to concern about side effects, they may worry that such drugs could lead to addiction. However, antipsychotic medications do not produce a "high" (euphoria) or addictive behavior in people who take them.

Another misconception about antipsychotic drugs is that they act as a kind of mind control, or a "chemical straitjacket." Antipsychotic drugs used at the appropriate dosage do not "knock out" people or take away their free will. While these medications can be sedating, and while this effect can be useful when treatment is initiated particularly if an individual is quite agitated, the utility of the drugs is not due to sedation but to their ability to diminish the hallucinations, agitation, confusion, and delusions of a psychotic episode. Thus, antipsychotic medications should eventually help an individual with schizophrenia to deal with the world more rationally.

Antipsychotic medications reduce the risk of future psychotic episodes in patients who have recovered from an acute episode. Even with continued drug treatment, some people who have recovered will suffer relapses. Far higher relapse rates are seen when medication is discontinued. In most cases, it would not be accurate to say that continued drug treatment "prevents" relapses; rather, it reduces their intensity and frequency. The treatment of severe psychotic symptoms generally requires higher dosages than those used for maintenance treatment. If symptoms reappear on a lower dosage, a temporary increase in dosage may prevent a full-blown relapse.

Because relapse of illness is more likely when antipsychotic medications are discontinued or taken irregularly, it is very important that people with schizophrenia work with their doctors and family members to adhere to their treatment plan. *Adherence* to treatment refers to the degree to which patients follow the treatment plans recommended by their doctors. Good adherence involves taking prescribed medication at the correct dose and proper times each day, attending clinic appointments, and/or carefully following other treatment procedures. Treatment adherence is often difficult for people with schizophrenia, but it can be made easier with the help of several strategies and can lead to improved quality of life.

There are a variety of reasons why people with schizophrenia may not adhere to treatment. Patients may not believe they are ill and may deny the need for medication, or they may have such disorganized thinking that they cannot remember to take their daily doses. Family members or friends may not understand schizophrenia and may inappropriately advise the person with schizophrenia to stop treatment when he or she is feeling better. Physicians, who play an important role in helping their patients adhere to treatment, may neglect to ask patients how often they are taking their medications, or may be unwilling to accommodate a patient's request to change dosages or try a new treatment. Some patients report that side effects of the medications seem worse than the illness itself. Further, substance abuse can interfere with the effectiveness of treatment, leading patients to discontinue medications. When a complicated treatment plan is added to any of these factors, good adherence may become even more challenging.

Strategies for Adherence

Fortunately, there are many strategies that patients, doctors, and families can use to improve adherence and prevent worsening of the illness. Some antipsychotic medications, including haloperidol (Haldol), fluphenazine (Prolixin), perphenazine (Trilafon) and others, are available in long-acting injectable forms that eliminate the need to take pills every day. A major goal of current research on treatments for schizophrenia is to develop a wider variety of long-acting antipsy-chotics, especially the newer agents with milder side effects, which can be delivered through injection. Medication calendars or pill boxes labeled with the days of the week can help patients and caregivers know when medications have or have not been taken. Using elec-tronic timers that beep when medications should be taken, or pairing medication taking with routine daily events like meals, can help patients remember and adhere to their dosing schedule. Engaging family members in observing oral medication taking by patients can help ensure adherence. In addition, through a variety of other meth-ods of adherence monitoring, doctors can identify when pill taking is a problem for their patients and can work with them to make adher-ence easier. It is important to help motivate patients to continue tak-ing their medications properly.

In addition to any of these adherence strategies, patient and family education about schizophrenia, its symptoms, and the medications being prescribed to treat the disease is an important part of the treat-ment process and helps support the rationale for good adherence.

What About Side Effects?

Antipsychotic drugs, like virtually all medications, have unwanted effects along with their beneficial effects. During the early phases of drug treatment, patients may be troubled by side effects such as drowsiness, restlessness, muscle spasms, tremor, dry mouth, or blur-ring of vision. Most of these can be corrected by lowering the dosage or can be controlled by other medications. Different patients have dif-ferent treatment responses and side effects to various antipsychotic drugs. A patient may do better with one drug than another.

The long-term side effects of antipsychotic drugs may pose a con-siderably more serious problem. Tardive dyskinesia (TD) is a disorder characterized by involuntary movements most often affecting the mouth, lips, and tongue, and sometimes the trunk or other parts of the body such as arms and legs. It occurs in about 15 to 20 percent of patients who have been receiving the older, "typical" antipsychotic drugs for many years, but TD can also develop in patients who have been treated with these drugs for shorter periods of time. In most cases, the symptoms of TD are mild, and the patient may be unaware of the movements.

Antipsychotic medications developed in recent years all appear to have a much lower risk of producing TD than the older, tradi-tional antipsychotics. The risk is not zero, however, and they can produce side effects of their own such as weight gain. In addition, if given at too high of a dose, the newer medications may lead to problems such as social withdrawal and symptoms resembling Parkinson's disease, a disorder that affects movement. Nevertheless, the newer antipsychotics are a significant advance in treatment, and their optimal use in people with schizophrenia is a subject of much current research.

What About Psychosocial Treatments?

Antipsychotic drugs have proven to be crucial in relieving the psychotic symptoms of schizophrenia—hallucinations, delusions, and incoherence—but are not consistent in relieving the behavioral symptoms of the disorder. Even when patients with schizophrenia are relatively free of psychotic symptoms, many still have extraordinary difficulty with communication, motivation, self-care, and establishing and maintaining relationships with others. Moreover, because patients with schizophrenia frequently become ill during the critical career-forming years of life (e.g., ages 18 to 35), they are less likely to complete the training required for skilled work. As a result, many with schizophrenia not only suffer thinking and emotional difficulties, but lack social and work skills and experience as well.

It is with these psychological, social, and occupational problems that psychosocial treatments may help most. While psychosocial approaches have limited value for acutely psychotic patients (those who are out of touch with reality or have prominent hallucinations or delusions), they may be useful for patients with less severe symptoms or for patients whose psychotic symptoms are under control. Numerous forms of psychosocial therapy are available for people with schizophrenia, and most focus on improving the patient's social functioning—whether in the hospital or community, at home, or on the job. Some of these approaches are described here. Unfortunately, the availability of different forms of treatment varies greatly from place to place.

Rehabilitation. Broadly defined, rehabilitation includes a wide array of non-medical interventions for those with schizophrenia. Rehabilitation programs emphasize social and vocational training to help patients and former patients overcome difficulties in these areas. Programs may include vocational counseling, job training, problem-solving and money management skills, use of public transportation, and social skills training. These approaches are important for the success of the community-centered treatment of schizophrenia, because they provide discharged patients with the skills necessary to lead productive lives outside the sheltered confines of a mental hospital.

Individual Psychotherapy. Individual psychotherapy involves regularly scheduled talks between the patient and a mental health professional such as a psychiatrist, psychologist, psychiatric social worker, or nurse. The sessions may focus on current or past problems, experiences, thoughts, feelings, or relationships. By sharing experiences with a trained empathic person—talking about their world with someone outside it—individuals with schizophrenia may gradually come to understand more about themselves and their problems. They can also learn to sort out the real from the unreal and distorted. Recent studies indicate that supportive, reality-oriented, individual psy-chotherapy, and cognitive-behavioral approaches that teach coping and problem-solving skills, can be beneficial for outpatients with schizophrenia. However, psychotherapy is not a substitute for antipsy-chotic medication, and it is most helpful once drug treatment first has relieved a patient's psychotic symptoms.

Family Education. Very often, patients with schizophrenia are dis-charged from the hospital into the care of their family; so it is impor-tant that family members learn all they can about schizophrenia and understand the difficulties and problems associated with the illness. It is also helpful for family members to learn ways to minimize the patient's chance of relapse—for example, by using different treatment adherence strategies—and to be aware of the various kinds of outpa-tient and family services available in the period after hospitalization. Family "psychoeducation," which includes teaching various coping strategies and problem-solving skills, may help families deal more effectively with their ill relative and may contribute to an improved outcome for the patient.

Self-Help Groups. Self-help groups for people and families dealing with schizophrenia are becoming increasingly common. Although not led by a professional therapist, these groups may be therapeutic because members provide continuing mutual support as well as com-fort in knowing that they are not alone in the problems they face. Self-help groups may also serve other important functions. Families working together can more effectively serve as advocates for needed research and hospital and community treatment programs. Patients acting as a group rather than individually may be better able to dispel stigma and draw public attention to such abuses as discrimination against the mentally ill.

Family and peer support and advocacy groups are very active and provide useful information and assistance for patients and families of patients with schizophrenia and other mental disorders.

How Can Other People Help?

A patient's support system may come from several sources, including the family, a professional residential or day program provider, shelter operators, friends or roommates, professional case managers, churches and synagogues, and others. Because many patients live with their families, the following discussion frequently uses the term "family." However, this should not be taken to imply that families ought to be the primary support system.

There are numerous situations in which patients with schizophre-nia may need help from people in their family or community. Often, a person with schizophrenia will resist treatment, believing that delu-sions or hallucinations are real and that psychiatric help is not required. At times, family or friends may need to take an active role in having them seen and evaluated by a professional. The issue of civil rights enters into any attempts to provide treatment. Laws protecting patients from involuntary commitment have become very strict, and families and community organizations may be frustrated in their efforts to see that a severely mentally ill individual gets needed help. These laws vary from State to State; but generally, when people are dangerous to themselves or others due to a mental disorder, the police can assist in getting them an emergency psychiatric evaluation and, if necessary, hospitalization. In some places, staff from a local community mental health center can evaluate an individual's illness at home if he or she will not voluntarily go in for treatment.

Sometimes only the family or others close to the person with schizophrenia will be aware of strange behavior or ideas that the person has expressed. Since patients may not volunteer such information during an examination, family members or friends should ask to speak with the person evaluating the patient so that all relevant information can be taken into account.

Ensuring that a person with schizophrenia continues to get treatment after hospitalization is also important. A patient may discontinue medications or stop going for follow-up treatment, often leading to a return of psychotic symptoms. Encouraging the patient to continue treatment and assisting him or her in the treatment process can positively influence recovery. Without treatment, some people with schizophrenia become so psychotic and disorganized that they cannot care for their basic needs, such as food, clothing, and shelter. All too often, people with severe mental illnesses such as schizophrenia end up on the streets or in jails, where they rarely receive the kinds of treatment they need.

How to Respond to Strange Statements

Those close to people with schizophrenia are often unsure of how to respond when patients make statements that seem strange or are clearly false. For the individual with schizophrenia, the bizarre beliefs or hallucinations seem quite real—they are not just "imaginary fantasies." Instead of "going along with" a person's delusions, family members or friends can tell the person that they do not see things the same way or do not agree with his or her conclusions, while acknowledging that things may appear otherwise to the patient.

It may also be useful for those who know the person with schizophrenia well to keep a record of what types of symptoms have appeared, what medications (including dosage) have been taken, and what effects various treatments have had. By knowing what symptoms have been present before, family members may know better what to look for in the future. Families may even be able to identify some "early warning signs" of potential relapses, such as increased withdrawal or changes in sleep patterns, even better and earlier than the patients themselves. Thus, return of psychosis may be detected early and treatment may prevent a full-blown relapse. Also, by knowing which medications have helped and which have caused troublesome side effects in the past, the family can help those treating the patient to find the best treatment more quickly.

In addition to involvement in seeking help, family, friends, and peer groups can provide support and encourage the person with schizophrenia to regain his or her abilities. It is important that goals be attainable, since a patient who feels pressured and/or repeatedly criticized by others will probably experience stress that may lead to a worsening of symptoms. Like anyone else, people with schizophrenia need to know when they are doing things right. A positive approach may be helpful and perhaps more effective in the long run than criticism. This advice applies to everyone who interacts with the person.

What Is the Outlook?

The outlook for people with schizophrenia has improved over the last 25 years. Although no totally effective therapy has yet been devised, it is important to remember that many people with the illness improve enough to lead independent, satisfying lives. As we learn more about the causes and treatments of schizophrenia, we should be able to help more patients achieve successful outcomes.

Studies that have followed people with schizophrenia for long periods, from the first episode to old age, reveal that a wide range of outcomes is possible. When large groups of patients are studied, certain factors tend to be associated with a better outcome—for example, a pre-illness history of normal social, school, and work adjustment. However, the current state of knowledge does not allow for a sufficiently accurate prediction of long-term outcome.

Given the complexity of schizophrenia, the major questions about this disorder—its cause or causes, prevention, and treatment—must be addressed with research. The public should beware of those offering "the cure" for (or "the cause" of) schizophrenia. Such claims can provoke unrealistic expectations that, when unfulfilled, lead to further disappointment. Although progress has been made toward better understanding and treatment of schizophrenia, continued investigation is urgently needed. As the lead Federal agency for research on mental disorders, NIMH conducts and supports a broad spectrum of mental illness research from molecular genetics to large-scale epidemiologic studies of populations. It is thought that this wide-ranging research effort, including basic studies on the brain, will continue to illuminate processes and principles important for understanding the causes of schizophrenia and for developing more effective treatments.

Psychosocial Rehabilitation and Recovery from Schizophrenia

Patrick A. McGuire

Treatment for schizophrenia has traditionally been based on the medical model, which emphasizes controlling and managing symptoms with medications. Psychosocial rehabilitation is an alternative approach that focuses on improving the individual's social and occupational skills. The underlying assumption behind psychosocial rehabilitation is that if people with schizophrenia are provided with social skills training, vocational counseling, and other social services, they can recover and live meaningful lives. Patrick A. McGuire cites research showing that psychosocial rehabilitation increases the likelihood of long-term recovery from schizophrenia. McGuire is a staff writer for the *APA Monitor*, a monthly publication of the American Psychological Association.

Early in 1999, when Ronald F. Levant, EdD, sought out colleagues to support an American Psychological Association (APA) miniconvention on serious mental illness, he told a group of fellow psychologists how recovery from a major disorder such as schizophrenia was not only possible, it was happening regularly.

"Recovery from schizophrenia?" a colleague snorted. "Have you lost your mind, too?"

Levant, APA's recording secretary and dean of the Center for Psychological Studies at Nova Southeastern University, was eventually able to rally support for the miniconvention, held in 1999 in Boston. But he still cringes at the sound of that laugh.

"I know psychologists who think that way about schizophrenia," he says. "I don't think they're up to speed. They don't know the literature. They haven't talked to consumers. Frankly, they are using models that are out of date."

The old treatment models, he notes, viewed patients as hopeless cases who needed to be stabilized with hospitalization, and then maintained with medications. The heavy, tranquilizing effects of those drugs made management of patients easier, although they only masked the disease. And, many now acknowledge, they caused serious side effects, including the familiar facial disfiguration known widely in the 1960s and '70s as "the Thorazine look."

"The old clinicians used to write about 'burned out schizophrenics,' like the burned out shell of a person," says psychologist Courtenay M. Harding, PhD, a professor of psychiatry at the University of Colorado. "But given half a chance, people can significantly improve or even recover."

In fact, among a small but growing core of psychologists—many of them, like Harding and Levant, members of an APA task force on serious mental illness—the concept of recovery, with its many definitions, is emerging as a new paradigm for schizophrenia treatment.

Psychologists are not only challenging the dire predictions of the past, they are finding new career paths as planners, teachers, counselors, managers, researchers, even public policy advocates. Many even see the schizophrenia field, once nearly barren of psychologists, as a promising market niche.

Defining "Recovery"

At the heart of the recovery movement is the idea that instead of focusing on the disease or pathological aspect of schizophrenia—as does the medical model—emphasis is placed on the potential for growth in the individual. That potential is then developed by integrating medical, psychological and social interventions.

Recovery, however, does not necessarily mean cure. Traditionally, the medical model of treatment has defined a "good outcome" from schizophrenia only in terms of a total cessation of symptoms, with no further hospitalization. Many who embrace the recovery paradigm feel those criteria are irrelevant.

"I define recovery as the development of new meaning and purpose as one grows beyond the catastrophe of mental illness," says William A. Anthony, PhD, executive director of Boston University's Center for Psychiatric Rehabilitation. "I think the literature on long-term studies . . . shows people do get past mental illness. My feeling is you can have episodic symptoms and still believe and feel you're recovering."

But even within the recovery movement, there are differing definitions of the term. Harding, for example, bases her view of recovery strictly on positive outcome research "findings," and not on the ongoing "process."

"In my definition there appears to be a recalibration of the brain to fully function again," she says. "I define recovery as reconstituted social and work behaviors, no need for meds, no symptoms, no need for compensation." Harding defines "significant improvement" as "someone who has recovered all but one of those areas."

Even with these differences, two key precepts of recovery have to do with a patient's right to play a hands-on role in getting well, and the need for the system to acknowledge that each patient is different and has different needs. That is unlike the old system, says Harding, where patients were treated with a "one-size-fits-all" approach, and if they didn't immediately get well, they were deemed forever chronic.

From past to present, experts have agreed on the general symptoms of schizophrenia—the hearing of voices, delusions, hallucinations, disorganized speech, confused thinking—but their efforts to trace its etiology have been stymied by the many forms the disease takes.

"Schizophrenia is a very loose concept," says Robert D. Coursey, PhD, a professor of psychology at the University of Maryland. "I once figured out that you could get 27 different profiles of people with schizophrenia using the *Diagnostic and Statistical Manual-IV (DSM-IV)*."

Today, an estimated 2.5 million Americans are diagnosed with schizophrenia. The National Institute of Health says the total costs of the illness approach $30 billion to $65 billion annually. Nearly a quarter of all mental illness costs combined are connected to schizo-phrenia, with two-thirds of its treatment costs borne by government.

On the human side, the statistics are equally grim: One of every 10 young males with schizophrenia commits suicide.

At the most optimistic of times, the traditional treatment paradigm conceded that perhaps 10 percent to 20 percent of those with schizo-phrenia might achieve recovery. But proponents of the recovery movement point to data that shows as high as a 68 percent rate of recovery and significant improvement.

The Elements of Psychosocial Rehabilitation

Best known under the name psychosocial rehabilitation, the recovery philosophy is practiced in about 4,000 dedicated programs across the country, says Ruth Hughes, PhD, president of the International Associ-ation of Psychosocial Rehabilitation Services (IAPRS). Each provides patients with work and social skills training, education about their dis-ease and why medications are important, symptom management, and often, therapy for dealing with the trauma of having schizophrenia.

They intervene in the acute stage of the disease by providing a nonthreatening place to go for symptom relief and crisis intervention, but they also work with those who have had schizophrenia for years, and haven't gotten well in other types of treatment. What makes these programs different from past treatments is the focus on a patient's potential, rather than the disease, and the closely coordi-nated integration of services across disciplines.

Oriented toward the practical, psychosocial rehabilitation teaches a patient how to access resources—such as health services and housing availability—and regain independent functioning. It also provides programs of enrichment or self-development, even basic support such as housing and food.

Another important tool in recovery, says Henry Tomes, PhD, APA's executive director for the public interest, is the psychosocial club-house. These are places, usually funded with local mental health funds and private donations, that focus primarily on teaching skills "that will lead people to live independently," says Tomes. "The primary goal is to allow people to work at competitive jobs."

Actual treatment for schizophrenia, he says, is obtained in other psychosocial programs outside the clubhouse.

All in all, says Coursey at Maryland, "A very large group of consumers has achieved remarkable recovery. They are people who, in spite of ongoing symptoms, have carved out a life. They have goals, they make choices, they improve their situation with the right type of interventions."

One of them is Ronald Bassman, PhD. Diagnosed with schizophrenia as a young man, he recovered, earned his doctorate and is now involved in patient empowerment programs in the New York State Office of Mental Health.

"It's miraculous how people come back," he says. "If you talk to someone who is doing better, he or she will tell you that someone—a friend, a family member, a pastor, a therapist—reached out with warmth and gentleness and kindness. This is not what is typically done in the mental health system."

To counter that, many former patients and their families have organized themselves as formidable advocates, calling themselves consumers, ex-patients and survivors. Their demand to be recognized as individuals who deserve a voice in their treatment is captured in the slogan "Nothing about us, without us."

In fact, their complaints have made them the significant factor in changing the system, say experts—and also in pointing up the failure of psychology to play a leadership role.

Where Are the Psychologists?

"Psychology as a field has not focused its training and teaching in the area of serious mental illness," says Anthony, in Boston. "This is a message that consumers have been bringing to us but we haven't been listening."

Too many psychologists, say Anthony and others, remain unaware of the new hope, and have shown little interest in working in schizophrenia.

"There is no one out there teaching patients how to cope with stressing voices," says Patricia Deegan, an ex-patient who is now director of training at the National Empowerment Center in Lawrence, Mass. "Or how to avoid or get out of the delusional vortexes of thought that you slide into. I think psychologists are a decade behind."

In fact, say survivors like Bassman and Deegan, valuable testimony from patients themselves is often dismissed.

"People say 'Oh, you were misdiagnosed,'" says Bassman. "Otherwise, you couldn't be where you are now.' I mean, that's an impossible circular argument."

Sadly, says Anthony Lehman, MD, a psychiatrist at the University of Maryland School of Medicine, "There is still a lot of mistrust in the professional community about patient self-reports. We just think 'Those people are crazy and they can't provide a valid assessment of what's going on in their lives.' I think we tend to discount people."

But it's not just the treatment system that has a blind spot.

According to Hughes at IAPRS, perhaps only one in 10 of the people who need psychosocial care for schizophrenia is getting it. A big reason for that, she says, is the reluctance of insurance companies to pay for anything but traditional treatment—which usually means medications alone.

"Most of those with schizophrenia are getting a maintenance approach that is not doing them a service," adds Lehman. "The evidence is that most people get fairly minimal treatment."

"What's really sad," says Harding, "is that [psychologists] could be really strong players in treatment and we're not."

Harding is best known for performing two of the longest longitudinal studies of schizophrenia outcomes in the United States. Her 1987 findings, viewed today by many as the centerpiece of the recovery movement, were the first empirical shots fired against the one-size-fits-all theory of that time.

Evidence of Recovery

Harding's research centered on a cohort of patients from the Vermont State Hospital, released between 1955 and 1960 in a state-funded, early model bio-psycho-social rehabilitation program. This was one of the first "deinstitutionalization" programs that emptied state hospitals across the country from the 1950s into the 1970s. Most relied solely on ex-patients taking powerful new psychotropic drugs to keep them stable on the outside.

The 269 patients chosen for the Vermont model study, however, were classic back ward cases—those diagnosed with chronic schizophrenia and deemed unable to survive outside.

Their 10-year rehabilitation program (1955–1965) relied on a team of caregivers including psychiatrists, a psychologist, a nurse, sociologists and a vocational counselor to maintain a continuity of care for the ex-patients. The team found community housing and provided vocational clinics that led to jobs, education and social supports, individualized treatment planning, as well as social skills training.

About two-thirds of the ex-patients did well, says Harding. When the model program ended, the cohort of ex-patients was already connected with natural community supports. Many of their original caregivers even checked in with them on a volunteer basis.

Harding entered the picture in the 1980s when she and her colleagues tracked down and interviewed all but seven of the original 269 patients—an average of 32 years after their first admission to the hospital.

"My clinical assessors and I were quite skeptical about finding any kind of recovery," she says, "because we'd all been trained in the old model. As a former psychiatric nurse on an inpatient unit, it sure didn't look like to me that anyone could get better."

Her methodology included a recalibration of the original diagnosis of each patient, using the current (1980) volume of the DSM-III. Its definition of schizophrenia was more restrictive than the volume published by the American Psychiatric Association in 1952. Those who interviewed the patients for Harding were blind to everything in the records, and the record abstracter was blind as to current outcome.

Not only did the rediagnoses of schizophrenia hold to the narrower definitions, Harding's study in *The American Journal of Psychiatry* (Vol. 144, No. 6, p. 718–735) showed that 62 percent to 68 percent of those former back ward patients showed no signs at all of schizophrenia. "They just didn't have them anymore."

But why? Harding suspected the psychosocial treatment program had made the difference, and got funding to conduct a comparison study to determine if that was true. She spent eight years looking for a similar cohort of patients and, with the help of colleague Michael DeSisto, PhD, as well as the Maine director of mental health, found a near-perfect match in the Augusta State Hospital in Maine.

"We matched each patient in Vermont to an Augusta patient," she says. "We matched everything. The age, the diagnosis, gender and the length of hospitalization. We matched the catchment areas on health and census data and all the protocols. We used DSM-III to do a rediagnosis on them. And matched the treatment era of the mid-1950s."

Only one thing did not match. In the years after their release, the ex-patients from Maine had not received any rehabilitation or systematic follow-up. The results: A significant improvement and recovery rate of 48 percent.

The Vermonters, says Harding, showed fewer symptoms, many more of them were working, and they showed much better community adjustment.

It dawned on her then that the Maine system and the Vermont system at the time were driven by very different treatment strategies.

"The Vermont model was self-sufficiency, rehabilitation and community integration," she recalls. "The Maine model was meds, maintenance and stabilization."

Even so, why did Vermont's strategy work better than Maine's? The answer reflects an intriguing aspect of the recovery movement: No one is quite sure why.

For instance, at Maryland, Coursey and his graduate students have conducted numerous interviews with people who have recovered from schizophrenia, asking them the same 'why' questions.

Many describe critical turning points.

They said the most important element "had been finding a safe, decent place to live, rather than being out on the streets," he says. "And a lot of these people in our studies had a mentor. Someone they trusted, who cared."

But why did that help?

"I think the 'why' is not that well understood," he says. "[Ex-patients] can describe what are the major elements, and we can see how they differ from those patients who give up. But what happened to make it happen is not always clear."

Even Anthony in Boston is not more specific.

"All of the interventions work in the context of a recovery vision," he says. "They each have their own particular goals. And combined together, they mysteriously help people recover."

Harding is more definite.

"The brain is the most plastic organ we have in interaction with the environment," she says. "Maybe what we are looking at is the neuroplasticity of the brain that is very slowly correcting the problem on its own, in interaction with the environment."

Does that mean people with schizophrenia will spontaneously recover at some point? Harding only smiles at the question, but notes that all of those in her Maine and Vermont studies who had fully recovered had long since stopped taking medications.

What they had in common was that they were out of the hospital, she says, "and had someone who believed in them, someone who had told them they had a chance to get better."

High Rates of Recovery

Harding's Vermont study was an immediate sensation because, while even skeptics agreed that from 10 percent to 20 percent of those with schizophrenia might recover, no one in the United States had ever suggested such a high rate of recovery, and in such a long-term study.

Also, Harding's results did not agree with the American Psychiatric Association's DSM-III, which explicitly said the prognosis for schizophrenia was uniformly poor.

"She was one of the researchers who dispelled many myths about long-term chronicity in mental illness," says Anthony, in Boston.

Harding cites nine other longitudinal studies like hers, conducted in Asia and Europe. Three of those were conducted before her 1987 study, but had been ignored by American researchers. Each of the nine studies reported an average of 50 percent or higher recovery rates. Hers was the only long-term pair of studies to be matched, and, say colleagues, was so expensive and time consuming that few others can afford to attempt a replication.

Some, though, even in the medical community, are conducting

more limited versions. Nancy Andreasen, MD, PhD, of the University of Iowa, for example, is just beginning to pull together the results of a longitudinal study, tracking patients with schizophrenia over 10 years.

"We see many patients who have improved substantially from their baseline diagnosis," she says. "Many patients emerge from the acute phase and stabilize, and then steadily improve."

Andreasen, a psychiatrist known for her research into the biological basis of human behavior in people with schizophrenia, agrees that the medical model is not the total answer to the question of treatment.

"Nobody believes more strongly than I that [treatment] should include psychological support and a decent effort to do psychosocial rehab," she says.

"Many of us feel that when you tell people their disease is lifelong, you may be creating self-fulfilling prophecies. There is empirical data accumulating that indicates the dire prognosis of schizophrenia we once had may not be so dire in many cases."

And, she adds, she and her colleagues in medicine and psychology "don't really know, scientifically, what the outcome is of schizophrenia in the era we live in—where patients are cared for in the community and treated with medications that have fewer side effects. We haven't really touched the surface of what we can do with psychosocial or cognitive rehabilitation. We need more of those programs."

True, says Levant at Nova Southeastern, but rehabilitation is only half the battle.

THE ROLE OF WORK IN REHABILITATION FROM SCHIZOPHRENIA

Tracy Thompson

In the following selection, *Washington Post* staff writer Tracy Thompson describes one man's experience with a psychosocial rehabilitation program—Green Door—that helped him find a job. Green Door is one of dozens of clubhouses for the mentally ill nationwide that provide members with opportunities to learn a skill, work on a volunteer basis, and eventually obtain a job in the competitive labor market, Thompson reports. The author contends that these programs play a crucial role in helping persons with schizophrenia and other severe mental illnesses to live ordinary lives.

Michael Raphael is awakened at 8 a.m. by the alarm clock in his bedroom in a row house on a noisy side street in Adams-Morgan [a Washington, D.C., neighborhood]. His mouth is cottony, and his need to sleep is so strong that waking up is like swimming to the surface under a waterfall. As usual, the twin bed across from his is empty; his roommate, Isaiah, has his own night life, which Michael doesn't know about, doesn't want to know. Aside from the two beds, the room contains a cheap armoire of a utilitarian design, a few of Michael's recently purchased knickknacks and some scattered clothes. No personality has imposed itself here; it is a room that belongs to no one.

Michael dresses himself carefully in his new clothes—white pants, a pale olive-green collarless shirt that he neatly buttons all the way up, shiny oxfords just out of their box, sunglasses. Then he takes his pills: one green and white, one yellow, three white. He goes downstairs and makes some coffee—his breakfast—spends some time talking with one of the men who live in the basement apartment, and looks at the cooking list posted on the refrigerator. Whose turn is it tonight? There are always arguments about that list. He'll probably end up doing the cooking again. What was that old saying? Everybody wanted to be king, nobody wanted to be an Indian. Or something like that.

Shortly after 10 a.m., it is time to go. Michael steps outside and closes the front door behind him. As he stands for a second on the steps of his group home, he looks entirely ordinary: a tall man with dark eyes, close-cropped hair, a mustache and a ready smile. He bounces on his toes a little as he goes down the steps; he knows he looks good today. He definitely feels good. Because for once, like almost everybody else on the street, he has somewhere to go. He has a job.

Attempting an Ordinary Life

Michael Raphael also has a mental illness. The name that should be assigned to it is unclear—not that it matters. As Harvard psychiatrist Robert Coles has written, "The labels psychiatrists use are merely matters of medical convenience." Over the years, the label doctors have attached to Michael's illness has changed from paranoid schizophrenia to what it is now—manic depression, also known as bipolar disorder. Schizophrenia is characterized by hallucinations, delusions, social withdrawal and a slowing of thought; manic depression features cycles of inert despair followed by spells of irritability, energy and, often, creativity. Despite the two illnesses' distinct array of symptoms, it can be tricky to tell them apart. Manic episodes can feature grandiose delusions that become psychotic; the passivity and withdrawal of schizophrenia often mimic depression. Over the years, Michael has had all these symptoms, and more.

And yet, despite these formidable odds, Michael is attempting to live an ordinary life—to hold down a paying job, to have fun on the weekends, maybe even someday move out of the group home and have his own place. He is 43 years old, and he has never quite managed an ordinary life, though he has made many attempts. But unlike his earlier attempts, this time may be different: He is on medication that controls his symptoms; he is doing well and will soon get his first paycheck working as a law office assistant in a transitional employment program. And he has a social support network to help him through the rough spots. Even with all that, this is an endeavor a bit like mountain-climbing with no rope and few tools, not knowing if there's enough oxygen to make it at a higher altitude. Years of illness have eroded his self-confidence and hampered his social skills. The drugs that help his brain to work leave him exhausted and worse, and must be taken with extreme care. Though he has held many jobs—briefly—he has little in the way of marketable experience. He has no car. He has nothing to fall back on: no savings account, no influential mentors. And looming over everything is the ever-present possibility of a relapse.

Michael tries not to dwell on what could go wrong, particularly today as he sets off down 16th Street. Just think about success! In a society where people sometimes go to outlandish lengths to proclaim their singularity, all Michael wants is to be like everybody else.

An Illness Reveals Itself

He was born James Emmett Gregory Jr. in May 1955 in a working-class neighborhood in Springfield, Massachusetts. A few years ago, he changed his name to Michael Gabriel Emmanuel Raphael because he felt it brought him closer to God. His father was a construction worker; his mother, a telephone operator. Both are now retired. Dorothy Gregory, who still lives in Springfield, remembers her first-born as an affectionate if somewhat reserved little boy who rarely missed a day of school and was liked by his teachers.

The thing that was waiting deep in the coils of Michael's brain revealed itself slyly, by stages—disguising itself at first as adolescent rebellion and moodiness. He quarreled with his parents and his sisters—there were five girls by the time he was 11—waging fierce battles so noisy that the neighbors could hear. In 10th grade, he began skipping school. He had always been a loner, but now the few friends he had fell away. Some mornings, his bed would be empty and he would be gone for days at a time. Once, he went to school in his pajamas. Another time, when he was 17, he left the house in a snowstorm—barefoot—and walked downtown. His mother became convinced drugs were at the root of her son's behavior—and in fact he was smoking pot and drinking. But those were symptoms, not the problem. At a local drug clinic, a man took Michael into a back room to talk to him. When the two emerged, the man told Michael's mother, "There's something bothering him, but I don't think it's drugs."

His parents checked Michael into a hospital, where he spent several months. When he got out, the local community mental health center helped him get an apartment and a roommate. By then, he was 18, legally an adult, and when he stopped going to counseling appointments or taking his medications, there was nothing his parents could do. His behavior again became erratic. He would go away, weeks would pass, and then there would be a phone call from him, saying he was stranded in New York City and could they please wire him money to get home?

The Army and Homelessness

He joined the Army. On the airplane to basic training, he began to think that he could read other people's thoughts. Radio waves filled his head, relayed by the fillings in his teeth. He could look at people sitting on a bench 50 feet away and hear what they were thinking. Usually, it was about him. He couldn't turn the noise off. Sometimes he would prop a book in his lap and pretend to read, but really he was just hiding, trying not to hear the babble, trying to figure out what to do. At other times he would break down and cry, and his drill instructor would say, "I'm going to make a man out of you yet." Then, one day, the instructor ordered him to pick up a rifle and he refused. The Army sent him for a psychiatric evaluation. The doctor asked him who the president was; he had no idea. The doctor asked him if he heard voices, and he said yes. So, the Army gave him a medical discharge, told him he was a paranoid schizophrenic, and sent him home.

For the next 25 years, Michael spent his time on the street, stumbling from Massachusetts to New York to Atlanta, a resident of homeless shelters, ratty hotels and halfway houses. Somewhere along the line, a social worker helped him qualify for Social Security disability payments, and he lived from check to check, sometimes taking medication, just as often not. He fended off thieves and sexual predators. For a while, he lived in a cardboard box. Once, he saw a homeless man sleeping on a traffic median get run over by a car and dragged to his death. Another time, he went to services at St. Patrick's Cathedral in New York City, where people glared at him because he stank. His friends and lovers were people in the same desperate circumstances; they came and went like clothes tumbling in a laundromat dryer.

Entering the Green Door

In 1997, he got on a train and wound up in Washington, D.C. On his first night here, he spent all the money he had—$140—on a hotel room, because he felt it was important to get a good night's sleep. After that, of course, he was back on the street—depressed, not taking his pills, growing increasingly suicidal. It was winter. He remembers a cab driver gave him a blanket. Somehow, he wound up at St. Elizabeth's Hospital, where he stayed for two months. When he was discharged, he was referred to yet another community mental health agency, this one called Green Door. And there, slowly and painfully, Michael began to reenter life.

Green Door is modeled on Fountain House in New York, an agency begun in 1948 by former psychiatric patients who pioneered the "clubhouse" concept for community psychiatric rehabilitation. Clubhouses have no "patients" or "clients," only "members," and there people with chronic mental illness can find a community that, depending on their health and level of motivation, can help them develop job skills. The goal is to help them find a paying job or, at least, a volunteer job to do at Green Door—to give them a sense of purpose.

A Green Door counselor got Michael a bed in a group home Green Door operates in Adams-Morgan. At first, Michael lived in the group home and wandered down 16th Street to the clubhouse one or two mornings a week. He would come in late in the morning, hang around for a few hours, bum some cigarettes, then go home. He was depressed, sleepy from the many pills he had to ingest, and unmotivated. Yet he kept telling the counselors that he wanted to work.

Weeks passed like this. Months. Then one day, Michael's counselor told him bluntly that it was time to put some action into his talk. I believe you can get a job, the counselor said, but you have to start showing up here every day on time. Show me you're serious.

Maybe it was the effect of regular medication, or his own willpower, or maybe Michael just needed somebody to tell him he could do it. He immediately went out and spent part of his Social Security check on an alarm clock. He started showing up regularly and on time. He began to make friends. He enrolled in Green Door's transitional employment program and began learning his way around basic office machinery. He listened when a counselor reminded him how to smile, make eye contact, shake hands. He found volunteer work to do at the clubhouse. And, eventually, he qualified for a part-time job at the David L. Bazelon Center for Mental Health Law on 15th Street. A real job in a real office.

Green Door became home, a source of support and sustenance. On this day, he goes there before his afternoon job at the Bazelon Center begins. Michael walks through Green Door's formal entryway and stops for a second. Off to the right in a parlor sit half a dozen members who are unable or unwilling to interact with the world. Michael doesn't go in there. A bunch of sleepyheads in that sleepyhead room. He used to sit there, too, but not anymore. He heads downstairs, to the cafe.

It might be a coffee bar anywhere—except that here, the patrons are, in some subtle way, different. On this day, one middle-aged man wears a too-tight shirt whose last button comes only to four inches above his navel, exposing a hairy belly. A slender woman quietly puts her head on the table and sits motionless. Another patron compliments the coffee in a too booming voice that temporarily brings all activity to a stop.

Michael doesn't notice; as he walks into the cafe he sees one of his friends, and, after a greeting, the two sit down together for a cup of coffee. Inside these walls, the world is fairly easy to understand. Outside, it is not so easy.

Weathering the Storm

Mental illness is like a storm in the brain. Drugs can make the storm abate or even disappear, but, like a beach after a hurricane, the brain still shows the damage. The long-term effects can include learned behaviors—bad habits, such as excessive passivity—as well as actual physical changes, which concentrate around basic cognitive processes: short-term memory, basic problem-solving skills, the way information is processed and organized. A person who has suffered for years from, say, schizophrenia can shop for groceries in a store he knows, but may be stumped when trying to buy lettuce in an unfamiliar store. He may be unable to ask for directions, or have forgotten the word "produce," or lost the ability to organize information into logical mental categories: Look for fresh vegetables, then look for something green. Then there are subtle social cues, like how close to stand to people, when to make eye contact, how much personal information to volunteer in a casual conversation, what to do with your hands, when to laugh—and when not to. For Michael, reentering the world after years of mental illness is, in some ways, like being at a country club where everybody knows the complex system of etiquette except him. This is not because he's stupid—no, surviving on the streets for 25 years, as he has, takes more than average smarts—but because his brain, after all these years, has taken quite a beating.

To help him negotiate this process, Michael has Margie Covarrubias. A tall woman of 49 with an enthusiastic manner and curly, iron-gray hair, Margie has agreed to meet Michael at 12:30 p.m. today outside Green Door's administrative offices, to accompany him to work. She wears black slacks, a plaid shirt and sensible shoes, and carries a Lands' End briefcase. As they walk together the few blocks to his new job, Michael discreetly lights his third cigarette of the day.

Since joining Green Door nearly four years ago, Margie has worked with several people like Michael. Some just need a boost to succeed. Others must be taught initiative; worn down by life to a state of resigned acceptance, they have learned to do exactly what they are told to do and no more. Some are inappropriately enthusiastic. Margie once found one trainee washing the metal legs of the conference room chairs with a bucket of soap and water because she thought they looked dusty.

Getting to Work

On the walk to the Bazelon Center, Michael and Margie make small talk—about whether he'll stop smoking, about the weather—and arrive just after 1 p.m. The center, which occupies a suite on the top floor of a downtown office building, is quiet; many of the staff lawyers are away from the office. Still, there is work to do: A pile of newsletters and press releases waits on the conference room table, ready to be organized and stuffed into envelopes. Also waiting is a young woman with extremely short hair and very dark lipstick, a Green Door member who is leaving the job to go on to something more permanent and who will help train Michael to take it over. Serious and subdued, her demeanor has an instant effect on Michael. He is like the new kid in class: He takes his cues from what he sees around him.

"Do you want me to collate?" he asks her. Margie, meanwhile, has stowed her briefcase under the table and taken a chair nearby, ready to answer questions or deal with unusual problems.

"Whatever you want," the short-haired woman replies. The two of them work without talking for nearly an hour, Michael assembling packages of material from various piles of fliers, the woman checking the packages for completeness and stuffing them into envelopes. Then it is time for Michael to learn the office system for sorting mail. He doesn't want to make a mistake. Not today. Better to take it slow.

And anyway, it is hard to figure out all the directions the woman is giving him when she says them only once. Michael feels a little bit like he is operating in a fog. . . .

As his shift wears on, Michael begins to relax. He smiles more, ventures a few jokes—some even at his own expense—talks about a car accident he once had and shows off the scars on the back of his head. He still looks at unfamiliar office machinery, though, as if it might be wired with explosives.

"I don't want to stick my hand in there," he says when the photocopier jams, stepping back as the short-haired woman stoops down to peer at the directions inside the machine. "I might not get it back." The woman, whose deadpan demeanor has not changed all afternoon, finally smiles and then figures out what the problem is. The machine starts working again. Soon it is time for a coffee break. Michael and the woman he will replace head downstairs and out the lobby door for a cigarette together.

Goals for the Future

Michael's goal is to be an executive secretary—maybe, he will say hopefully, even in the White House. Why not? One year ago, he was living on the street; who would have imagined then that he would be where he is now? It's an improbable dream. On the other hand, maybe the real dream has been the last 25 years. Sometimes, running memories through his head, it's as if someone else was in his body doing all those odd things—walking barefoot in a winter blizzard, hearing the private thoughts of a stranger at a bus stop. "I look back and say, 'I did that?'" he says in wonderment. Yet his attitude toward his illness is ambiguous. Speaking of things he did as a teenager, he says, "People thought I was cuckoo, and I was." Later, though, he says that he never really thought he was mentally ill, that he just went along with the doctors' diagnosis to qualify for Social Security disability payments. And at another point, he blames his mental problems on smoking pot and drinking as a teenager. If he hadn't done those things, he would never have had any problems.

But he did, and now a quarter of a century has passed. His mother is old, and undergoing treatment for breast cancer. All Michael can do is worry, and call her when he can. Each time, he tells her he loves her. It makes his mother happy to hear from him, but she is also a little wary. It's never been smooth. Michael doesn't talk to his father, and his sisters get news of him through their mother. To them, he's never been anything but trouble, and they have families of their own now.

Sometimes, he thinks about how he might have had a home and children of his own now, too, if he'd never been ill. It makes him sad. He doesn't like to talk about it much. Still, there are fleeting glimpses of his longing. Tidying up the Bazelon Center conference room after he finishes getting the stack of newsletters ready to be mailed,

Michael says, apropos of nothing, that he lived with a woman once, back in Massachusetts. The woman had a small child, he said. "That's a sweet thing, that family life. Just sitting there and watching the TV." He shakes his head, smiling. "Boy, that's sweet."

Soon, it's almost 5 p.m., time for the last task of the day: collecting the mail, separating whatever needs to be sent by Express Mail, putting it all in a bin and taking it downstairs to the building's main mail collection point. The short-haired woman shows Michael how that is done. Now that he's feeling more comfortable, it's easy enough to figure out. It's a relief. The end of the day and no major blunders. Outside, the short-haired woman says good night and goes her way. Margie lingers for a moment. She will be back; Michael will need someone with him on the job for another two weeks, she figures.

It's still early; blank evening hours lie ahead. Michael would like to find a cheap place to eat in Adams-Morgan—kind of a celebration—but it's the last day of the month. The Social Security check won't be credited to his bank account until midnight, and he has not gotten his first week's pay of $125 yet. Hang in there, Margie tells him; you're doing great.

"I've changed," Michael tells her. "I look in the mirror now sometimes and say, 'Wow.'" She reaches out and briefly touches his arm. Then he turns and heads north on 15th Street, back to Adams-Morgan and the group home and an evening of whatever is on hand for dinner, maybe some television, taking his pills and then bed. It's a life. Maybe even an ordinary life.

PSYCHOTHERAPY CAN HELP PEOPLE WITH SCHIZOPHRENIA

Denise Grady

In recent decades, medication has been considered superior to psychotherapy as a treatment for schizophrenia. However, Denise Grady explains, while medication can help to control symptoms, people with schizophrenia often need additional assistance dealing with stress and interpersonal relationships. Grady describes two studies suggesting that a certain type of psychotherapy—called "personal therapy"—benefits people with schizophrenia. Personal therapy, which focuses on stress management and social skills, was shown to improve the personal relationships and work performance of people with schizophrenia, she concludes. Grady writes on health issues for the *New York Times*.

When a man with schizophrenia requested psychotherapy recently in addition to his antipsychotic medication, he was told that his health maintenance organization would allow only six sessions. "The insurer said there was no evidence that psychotherapy helps people with schizophrenia," said Gerard Hogarty, a researcher and professor of psychiatry at the University of Pittsburgh School of Medicine.

The story is all too familiar to therapists. The notion behind it is that people with schizophrenia are either too sick to be reached by psychotherapy or, thanks to medication, too well to need it.

But Professor Hogarty and his research team have shown that schizophrenic patients taking medication can be helped further by a certain type of psychotherapy. In two studies published in November 1997 in *The American Journal of Psychiatry*, the group showed that a three-year course of the treatment, which they developed and named personal therapy, was extremely helpful to many patients in preventing relapses and improving social adjustment.

Dr. Wayne Fenton, medical director of Chestnut Lodge Hospital in Rockville, Md., who was an author of an editorial accompanying the results of the studies, said they provided the first scientific proof that psychotherapy can help people with schizophrenia. "Because of this, people can no longer argue that psychotherapy for schizophrenia is not effective," Dr. Fenton said. "One might say there is no excuse anymore not to provide needed care."

"Better, but Not Well"

Although antipsychotic drugs are unmatched in their power to halt the hallucinations and delusions that characterize schizophrenia, they do not erase all signs of illness.

"People are better, but not well," Professor Hogarty said. Despite medication, many patients still have difficulties with memory, attention, problem solving and relating to other people. Relapses are common, often because patients quit taking their medication, but sometimes even when they stick with it. Only 10 percent to 30 percent of the two million Americans with schizophrenia are employed. "There's no drug out there to teach you how to get along with anybody, or how to get a job and keep one," Professor Hogarty said.

Dr. George T. Niederehe, head of the adult and geriatric psychosocial treatment research program at the National Institute of Mental Health, said, "Many of the people we talk about as the homeless are persons with these kinds of mental health problems."

Dr. Niederehe and other experts praised the study. "It's a major advance," said Dr. William T. Carpenter Jr., director of the Maryland Psychiatric Research Center in Baltimore. Dr. Carpenter, who was not associated with the study, said that personal therapy appeared to be the most beneficial treatment developed since the first antipsychotic drugs were introduced in the 1950's.

The treatment of schizophrenia has had a contentious history. When it became clear during the 1960's that antipsychotic drugs worked far better than psychotherapy for most patients, doctors began to question whether psychotherapy was of any use for people with schizophrenia. There are about 400 different types of psychotherapy, Professor Hogarty said, and studies in the last 30 years have been contradictory, with some finding psychotherapy helpful in treating schizophrenia and others calling it useless or even harmful.

Personal Therapy

By the mid-1980's, psychotherapy had such a bad reputation among experts in schizophrenia that a proposal to study anything by that name would have been "an invitation to unemployment," Professor Hogarty said. The climate inspired him and his colleagues to call the techniques they developed something else: personal therapy.

Their treatment differs radically from the Freudian psychoanalysis that many people think of as psychotherapy. "We're not looking into suppressed thoughts about Mama," Professor Hogarty said. "It's more in the here and now."

Personal therapy is based on the idea that people with schizophrenia are born with brain abnormalities that make them especially vulnerable to emotional stress. Overwhelming stress, often from dealings with other people, can lead to anxiety and depression, which may in turn spiral down into psychosis.

In personal therapy, the therapist tries initially to help patients recognize stress and manage it in order to avoid relapses of schizophrenia. The treatment program is tailored to each patient's needs, and patients progress at their own pace. Eventually, they may reach a stage where they are ready for counseling to help them get along better with other people and to minimize stressful encounters.

Professor Hogarty's study included 151 patients, 97 living with their families and 54 living independently. Most were in their 20's or 30's, and all took antipsychotic medication. Each was assigned to a group that received personal therapy two to four times a month for three years, or, for comparison, family therapy, personal and family therapy, or supportive therapy in which patients were given the opportunity to talk with a therapist and seek help during crises.

In the patients who lived with relatives, only a quarter who received personal therapy alone had relapses, as opposed to half of those who had the other kinds of therapy. Only two quit personal therapy, but 13 dropped out of the other programs.

But in patients living on their own, more receiving personal therapy had relapses than those getting supportive treatment: about half relapsed, as opposed to slightly more than a third of the others. Four left personal therapy, and five left supportive therapy. The researchers said they suspected that personal therapy failed in that group because many of the patients were struggling to find housing, food and clothing, and the treatment may have been too demanding for them.

But in another area, social adjustment, both groups of patients benefited from personal therapy. Personal relationships and work performance improved. Most important, they continued to get better over time, while benefits from the other types of therapy tended to reach a plateau after a year. Had the study gone on, Professor Hogarty said, the patients in personal therapy might have continued to improve even further.

Cognitive Enhancement Therapy

He and his team have devised another treatment that they are now testing, called cognitive enhancement therapy. It involves computer programs aimed at helping patients improve problem-solving skills, and group sessions designed to heighten the ability to act wisely in social situations. Patients like it, and Professor Hogarty thinks the treatment may ultimately prove even more helpful than personal therapy.

Despite the value of personal therapy, other researchers and Professor Hogarty himself said they doubted it would come into widespread use. It is expensive and time-consuming, and would require extensive retraining of therapists.

Nonetheless, Professor Hogarty said, in the long run personal therapy might prove cost effective, because by preventing relapses it can
keep patients out of the hospital, which is the most expensive form of
care. The treatment may also get them back in the work force. "You
get what you pay for," he said. "If you want to pay something more,
the lives of these patients can improve substantially."

A CRITIQUE OF PSYCHIATRY'S TREATMENT OF SCHIZOPHRENIA

Al Siebert

In the following selection, Al Siebert argues that psychiatrists are too quick to label patients as "schizophrenic" and too eager to convince them that they are mentally ill. In addition, according to Siebert, psychiatrists misrepresent the facts about schizophrenia to the public by incorrectly insisting that it is a brain disease from which recovery is rare. Siebert contends that people with symptoms of schizophrenia would be better served if professionals merely listened to them rather than labeling them schizophrenic and attempting to persuade them that they have a brain disease. Siebert, who received a Ph.D. in clinical psychology from the University of Michigan, is a retired college teacher and the author of several books.

When I was a staff psychologist at a neuropsychiatric institute in 1965, I conducted an experimental interview with an 18-year-old woman diagnosed as "acute paranoid schizophrenic." I'd been influenced by the writings of Carl Jung, Thomas Szasz, and Ayn Rand and was puzzled about methods for training psychiatric residents that are unreported in the literature. I prepared for the interview by asking myself questions. I wondered what would happen if I listened to the woman as a friend, avoided letting my mind diagnose her, and questioned her to see if there was a link between events in her life and her feelings of self-esteem. My interview with her was followed by her quick remission. . . .

My duties as a staff psychologist at the Neuropsychiatric Institute at the University of Michigan Hospital in 1965 included attending morning "rounds." The staff gathered in a small conference room at 7:30 a.m. to hear various announcements and reports about patient admissions and discharges.

One morning, the head nurse of the locked ward reported the admission of an 18-year-old woman. The psychiatric resident who admitted her the previous evening said, "Molly's parents brought her in. They told us Molly claims God talked to her. My provisional diag-

Excerpted from "How Non-Diagnostic Listening Led to a Rapid 'Recovery' from Paranoid Schizophrenia: What Is Wrong with Psychiatry?" by Al Siebert, *Journal of Humanistic Psychology*, Winter 2000. Reprinted with permission from the author.

Ron: My wife and family say I don't think right. (clenches jaw) They say I talk crazy. They pressured me into this place.

A.S.: (Al Siebert): You're a voluntary admission, aren't you?

Ron: Yes. It won't do any good though; they're the ones who need a psychiatrist.

A.S.: Why do you say that?

Ron: I work in sales in a big company. Everyone there is out for themselves. I don't like it. I don't like to pressure people or trick them into buying to put bucks in my pocket. The others seem to go for it . . . selfish, clawing to get ahead. I tried to talk to my boss, but he says I have the wrong attitude. He rides me all the time.

A.S.: So what is the problem with your family?

Ron: I've talked about quitting and going to veterinarian school. I like animals. I'd like that work. My wife says I'm not thinking right. She wants me to stay with the company and work up into management. She went to my parents and got them on her side.

We talked for a while about how his wife and parents wanted him to live up to their dreams for him. I said, "I still don't see the reason for your being here."

Ron: They're upset because I started yelling at them how selfish they are. My wife wants a husband who earns big money, owns a fancy home, and drives an expensive car. She doesn't want to be the wife of a veterinarian. They can't see how selfish they are in trying to make me fit into a slot so they can be happy. Everyone is telling me what I should think and what should make me happy.

A.S.: So you told them how selfish they are?

Ron: Yes. They couldn't take it because they believe they are only interested in my welfare. (He sagged in his chair and held his face in his hands.)

A.S.: Did you tell the admitting physician about them trying to make you think right?

Ron: Yes. Everyone is trying to brainwash me. My wife, my parents, the sales manager. Everyone is trying to push their thinking into my head.

A.S.: How do you feel about all this?

Ron: I feel angry. They say they have done this to help me, but they don't care about me. They're all selfish. Afraid I'll upset their tight little worlds. I shouldn't be here.

I saw that Ron's doctor was obediently acting as trained when he diagnosed Ron as paranoid. The consequence, however, was a "crazy-making" double-bind for Ron. His doctor was saying to him, in essence, "Because you believe that people are trying to force thoughts into your mind, you must accept into your mind the thought that you are mentally ill."

Two days later, Ron signed out. It was rumored that he took off for California.

These incidents helped me see how hard psychiatrists try to force their words and thoughts into patients' minds without insight into what they are doing. When a patient disagrees, this is diagnosed as "resistance" or "lack of insight" and viewed as another sign of "mental illness."

Diagnosis vs. Understanding

3. During admissions meetings, I had observed that when a patient was reported as talking in bizarre ways, the staff would reflexively declare the person "schizophrenic." Diagnosis seemed more important than understanding. No one seemed influenced by Carl Jung, who said in his autobiography,

> Through my work with the patients I realized that paranoid ideas and hallucinations contain a germ of meaning. . . . The fault is ours if we do not understand them. . . . It was always astounding to me that psychiatry should have taken so long to look into the content of the psychoses.

4. I had just finished Ayn Rand's book *Atlas Shrugged* (1957). I was impressed with her portrayal of how the need for self-esteem influences what people do, say, think, and feel. I'd been noticing, for example, that when someone made a statement of extremely high self-esteem, most people reacted negatively and tried to tear the person down. I wondered what was wrong with thinking highly of oneself.

My Questions

As I prepared myself for my interview with Molly the next day, I developed four questions for myself:

What would happen if I just listened to her and did not allow my mind to put any psychiatric labels on her?

What would happen if I talked to her believing that she could turn out to be my best friend?

What would happen if I accepted everything she reports about herself as being the truth?

What would happen if I questioned her to find out if there is a link between her self-esteem, the workings of her mind, and the way that others have been treating her?

The Interview with Molly

The next morning, I took my Wechsler Adult Intelligence Scale testing kit and Bender-Gestalt cards with me to the ward. I laid out the materials on a table in the dining room and waited until the nurse brought Molly in.

Molly was about average height and looked slightly overweight. Her shoulders slumped forward. She was a plain-looking young woman wearing no makeup. Her straight, light brown, shoulder-length hair needed washing. She wore a loose, faded, cotton dress. Dowdy was the word that came to mind.

When the nurse introduced us, Molly glanced quickly at me. She did not say anything, even though I could feel her attention on me. She seemed frightened and lonely.

I seated her at the end of a table and I sat at the side. Instead of trying to talk with her, I put her to work copying Bender-Gestalt designs onto sheets of paper. She cooperated and did what I asked.

I was not especially interested in how well she could draw; I just wanted her to become comfortable with me. I sat, relaxed and quiet. When she finished a drawing, I would say, "Good," "That's fine" or "Okay, here's the next one."

When she finished the drawings, I started her on the Wechsler block design test. She followed instructions accurately and worked at a good speed. I could see that she was not depressed and had no obvious neurological problems.

She gradually warmed up to me, and she relaxed as we proceeded. After about 15 minutes, she peeked out from under her hair and looked cautiously into my eyes.

At the first moment of good eye contact, I smiled and said "Hello."

She blushed and ducked her head.

I felt a rapport with her and felt that I could start a conversation. It went like this:

A.S. (Al Siebert): Molly? (She looks up at me.) I am curious about something. Why are you here in a psychiatric hospital?

Molly: God spoke to me and said I was going to give birth to the second Savior.

A.S.: That may be, but why are you here in this hospital?

Molly: (startled, puzzled) Well, that's crazy talk.

A.S.: According to whom?

Molly: What?

A.S.: Did you decide when God spoke to you that you were crazy?

Molly: Oh. No. They told me I was crazy.

A.S.: Do you believe you are crazy?

Molly: No. But I am, aren't I? (dejected)

A.S.: If you will put that in the form of a question, I'll answer you.

Molly: (slightly puzzled, pauses to think) Do you think I am crazy?

A.S.: No.

Molly: But that couldn't have happened, could it?

A.S.: As far as I am concerned, you are the only person who knows what happens in your mind. Did it seem real at the time?

Molly: Oh yes!

A.S.: Tell me what you did after God spoke to you.

Molly: What do you mean?

A.S.: Did you start knitting booties and sweaters and things?

Molly: (laughs) No, but I did pack my clothes and wait by the door several times.

A.S.: Why?

Molly: I felt like I would be taken someplace.

A.S.: It wasn't where you expected, was it?

Molly: (laughing) No!

A.S.: One thing I'm curious about.

Molly: What?

A.S.: Why is it that of all women in the world, God chose you to be the mother of the second Savior?

Molly: (breaks into a big grin) You know, I've been trying to figure that out myself!

A.S.: I'm curious. What things happened in your life before God spoke to you?

Molly's Story

It took about 30 minutes to draw out her story. Molly was an only child who had tried unsuccessfully to earn love and praise from her parents. They only gave her a little love once in a while, just enough to give her hope she could get more. She voluntarily did many things around the house, such as cooking and cleaning. Her father had been a musician so she joined the school orchestra. She thought this would please him. She practiced hard, and the day she was promoted to first chair in the clarinet section, she ran home from school to tell her father. She expected him to be very proud of her, but his reaction was to smash her clarinet across the kitchen table and tell her, "You'll never amount to anything."

After graduation from high school, Molly entered nursing school. She chose nursing because she believed that in the hospital, the patients would appreciate the nice things she would do for them. She was eager and excited about her first clinical assignment, but it turned into a shattering experience. The two women patients she was assigned to criticized her. She could not do anything right for them. She felt "like the world fell in." She ran away from school and took a bus to the town where her high school boyfriend was in college. She went to see him, but he told her to go home and write to him. He said they could still be friends, but he wanted to date other girls.

A.S.: How did you feel after that?

Molly: Awful lonely.

A.S.: So your dad and mom didn't love you, the patients were critical and didn't like you, and your boyfriend just wanted to be friends. That made you feel very sad and lonely.

Molly: (head down, dejected) Yes, there didn't seem to be anyone in the whole world who cared for me at all.

A.S.: And then God spoke to you.

Molly: Yes. (quietly)

A.S.: How did you feel after God gave you the good news?

Molly: (looks up, smiles warmly at me) I felt like the most special person in the whole world.

A.S.: That's a nice feeling, isn't it?

Molly: Yes, it is.

(The kitchen crew came into the dining room to set up for lunch.)

A.S.: I must go now.

Molly: Please don't tell them what we've been talking about. No one seems to understand.

A.S.: I know what you mean. I promise not to tell if you won't.

Molly: I promise.

"Spontaneous Remission"?

Two days later, I was walking through the locked ward to see another patient. When Molly saw me, she walked over and stopped me by putting her hand on my arm. "I've been thinking about what we talked about," she said. "I've been wondering. Do you think I imagined God's voice to make myself feel better?"

She surprised me. I did not intend to do therapy, but she seemed to see the connection. I paused. I thought to myself, "Maybe so. But if there is an old-fashioned God who does things like this, then He is watching! I don't care what the other doctors and nurses do, I am not going to give her a rough time. I am going to be her friend!" I shrugged my shoulders. I said "perhaps" and smiled at her. She smiled back with good eye contact, then turned and walked away.

At staff rounds, the head nurse reported a dramatic improvement in Molly. She was now a cheerful, talkative teenager. She spoke easily with her doctor, the nurses, and other patients. She started participating in patient activities. She brushed and combed her hair, put on makeup, and asked for nicer looking dresses.

At rounds a week later, Dr. Bostian described her amazing recovery as "a case of spontaneous remission." The plans to commit her were dropped. A few days later, she was transferred to the open ward and she did so well that the doctors and nurses expected her to be discharged soon. I left the hospital soon after, so I was not able to follow up. What would have happened to her if I had not taken time to listen to her with an open mind and affirm her reality? The psychiatric staff's prediction that she would spend many years in the back ward of the state hospital would most likely have been validated.

Important Questions

One expects mental health professionals to be exemplary models of mental health. This would include being open-minded about new and better ways to be effective and receptive to constructive feedback. But, just as the writings of Thomas Szasz have been rejected and dismissed by mainstream psychiatry for over three decades, my efforts to have this account of my interview with "Molly" published in a professional journal were, until now, unsuccessful for more than 30 years. . . .

There is ample evidence that something is wrong with psychiatry. It is predictable, for example, that current experts on "schizophrenia" will declare that the psychiatric staff at the University of Michigan Hospital made an incorrect diagnosis of Molly, that she was not really "schizophrenic," and that she is not representative of "schizophrenic" patients who end up in mental hospitals. The key to significant progress with "schizophrenia" may be to stop looking at what "mental health" practitioners think about their patients and to look at how the practitioners themselves think. Important research questions would include the following:

Why is the psychiatric literature silent about why psychiatric residents must try to make patients believe they are mentally ill?

A related issue is lack of insight that psychiatrists have about incongruent "mixed messages" in their actions and words. A psychiatrist will, in effect, say to a person diagnosed as delusional, "Because you believe that people are trying to force thoughts into your mind, you must accept into your mind the thought that you are mentally ill." The psychiatrist is unaware that he or she is doing the very thing he or she is declaring is not happening. This is a "crazy-making" experience for psychiatric patients.

When someone diagnosed as schizophrenic disagrees that he or she is ill, why does the psychiatric profession insist that the person "lacks insight"? . . .

What are the cognitive processes in the mind of a person perceiving "schizophrenia" in someone else?

Why does the thought, "That's schizophrenic," get triggered in the minds of clinicians when they hear a person reveal certain thoughts and feelings? Why is a disturbing person perceived as "disturbed"? Is the perception of "schizophrenia," in part, a stress reaction in the mind of the beholder?

Why does the psychiatric profession feel compelled to "treat" people diagnosed as having "schizophrenia" when, after 100 years of clinical experience and research, there is still no proof in the psychiatric literature that what is called "schizophrenia" is a medical disease with demonstrable neurophysiological dysfunction? . . .

Why do psychiatrists who specialize in schizophrenia misrepresent what is known about schizophrenia to the public?

Prominent schizophrenia psychiatrists such as Nancy Andreasen, editor-in-chief of the *American Journal of Psychiatry*, David Pickar, chief of the experimental therapeutics branch of the National Institutes of Mental Health, and E. Fuller Torrey have stated in national broadcast interviews that schizophrenia is a brain disease like Alzheimer's, Parkinson's, or multiple sclerosis. These statements are inconsistent, however, with research facts and scientific evidence. . . .

When Kaid Farhn was arrested in December 1998 for nearly chok-
ing to death a 3-year-old girl standing with her mother in a Brooklyn
subway station, it did not make news. He was recently found unfit to
stand trial and confined for treatment—the second time in two years.
In 1997, Farhn was arrested for assaulting three people, judged unfit
and sent to the state psychiatric hospital on Staten Island, where,
according to state documents, he was released after three weeks.

There are now far more mentally ill in the nation's jails and prisons
(200,000) than in state hospitals (61,700). With 3,000 mentally ill
inmates on Rikers Island, the New York City jail is now, in effect, the
state's largest psychiatric facility. In a year's time, according to a study
by the Urban Justice Center, 15,000 prisoners in Rikers are treated for
serious mental illness.

Some, like Goldstein, are awaiting trial on violent crimes. But far
more have been too sick to cope alone in the community and were
arrested for shoplifting, disturbing the peace, public lewdness, intoxi-
cation, drug use, fare-beating. Many would never have landed behind
bars if there were adequate community care.

And that is the larger, quieter scandal behind the states' failure.
While some of the untreated are dangerous, far more suffer unneces-
sarily from their own illnesses. After years of declining numbers, the
population of homeless adults is rising again in New York City shelters; it is estimated that of the 7,200 homeless, 2,200 to 3,000 are
mentally ill. These days, commuters are noticing more disoriented
people begging on the city's subways; police precinct commanders
report a growth in "E.D.P." (emotionally disturbed persons) cases.
"The number of disturbed people out there is definitely creeping back
up," says Mary Brosnahan, director of the Coalition for the Homeless
in New York City.

A Return to the 1840's

On a winter's night, I visited the city's Atlantic Avenue shelter in
Brooklyn—a run-down, dark, drafty military armory that houses 300
men. It is a mean, hard place; the previous shelter manager was
assaulted there and never returned to work. Everywhere disoriented
men were talking to themselves, staring into space, rocking back and
forth, their faces hidden like shades in hooded sweatshirts. A man
with mangy hair, a foul smell and red plaid pants walked up to a top-
ranking city official and explained that he was Albert Einstein. "I'm
paranoid," Einstein said. "I think I did something I didn't do."

To Muzzy Rosenblatt, then the city's Acting Commissioner of
Homeless Services, it is the mental-health system that seems crazy.
"We shouldn't have mentally ill people in our shelters," he says.
"They should be in mental-health programs."

The state's Commissioner of Mental Health under Governor Pataki
is James Stone, and advocates for the mentally ill have been so frus-

trated by his department's failure to finance more community-housing programs that they bitterly refer to this period as "the Stone Age." Indeed, in some ways we are back to where we were in the 1840's, when the legendary reformer Dorothea Dix set out to shame Massachusetts legislators into doing something for the mentally ill, who were locked away in the basements of local almshouses and jails. In 1843, Dix completed a 32-page expose, "Memorial to the Massachusetts Legislature": "I proceed, Gentlemen, briefly to call your attention to the present state of Insane Persons confined within this Commonwealth in cages, closets, stalls, pens! Chained, naked, beaten with rods and lashed into obedience!"

Dix described the care of each mentally ill person she had seen: "Saugus poorhouse: Apartment entirely unfurnished; no chair, table, nor bed . . . cold, very cold. . . . On the floor sat a woman, her limbs immovably contracted, so that the knees were brought upward to the chin; the face was concealed, the head rested on the folded arms." Her accounts reminded me of the basement apartment in Brooklyn where Andrew Goldstein lived, as described in Jamaica Hospital records: "One-room unit, nonfunctioning bathroom, unsafe electrical wires hanging from ceiling, no electricity, foul smell of dead and decaying mice, lock to room broken. In general, conditions unsuitable for living."

Though a moralist, Dix understood that it was all about money, as David Gollaher points out in his biography of her, *Voice for the Mad*. The 1840 Massachusetts census counted 978 "lunatics"; the two state asylums had only 353 beds. The state, Dix implored, must appropriate $60,000 to create beds for the 625 neglected; cities and towns were too small and too poor to finance their own asylums, she argued. Shamed into it, Massachusetts found the money. And that was what cemented the states' responsibility for the seriously mentally ill. . . .

Impressive Community Treatment Models

In the early 1990's, I spent two years all but living at a well-run, state-financed group home for a book on the mentally ill. What I saw made me a believer in quality community programs and in the nonprofit agencies that use state money to run them. There were problems at the home, but they did not spill into the streets, because counselors were there to defuse the crises.

Today there is an impressive array of state-financed community models, from the heavily regimented to the lightly supervised, that have been developed by nonprofits: group homes for mentally ill substance abusers that use an abstinence model and have 24-hour supervision; S.R.O.'s, where people have their own rooms, share kitchens and get support from caseworkers and psychiatrists with offices on the premises; rent-subsidy programs to pay for an apartment in an affordable building in the community, with a case manager who might visit as often as every day or as rarely as once a month.

The programs are so varied because the needs of the mentally ill vary, too. Among the least restrictive is Pathways to Housing, a program based in Harlem and Queens, which gives homeless mentally ill people who have long resisted treatment apartments even if they still have a drinking or drug problem and do not want to take medication. They are assigned a case manager who sees them regularly, making sure their problems with meds or substance abuse are reasonably under control. Though many Pathways residents had been homeless for more than a decade, 88 percent were still housed in this program after five years.

Thayer Gamble, 43, is one. Talk about a time bomb: he is schizophrenic, was suicidal, used crack and has been imprisoned several times. Four years ago a hospital social worker referred him to Pathways, which gave him an apartment and a caseworker, Ben Tallerson. Tallerson visited Gamble's Harlem apartment regularly. Because Tallerson knew Gamble, he realized one reason Gamble had trouble taking his medication properly. "He can't read," Tallerson says. "He didn't know what it meant to take meds A.M. and P.M." Tallerson drew it out for him, the sun for A.M., the moon for P.M. And two years ago, when Gamble started on crack again, Tallerson noticed. "When Thayer's going good," he says, "he has clean habits, he keeps himself clean, his apartment is clean. Now I start seeing his physical appearance is sloppy, he's smelly, he's hanging on the streets." Tallerson urged him into a detox program. As Gamble says, "I have his beeper number—if I'm having a problem at 3:30 in the morning, I can call Ben."

There are thousands of mentally ill New Yorkers whose lives are better because of state-financed programs like Pathways—it's just that success is less visible than failure. Cecil Dozier, 44, panhandled at the corner of Bleecker and Thompson in Greenwich Village in the fall of 1998. He is now in a program for mentally ill substance abusers run by Volunteers of America. Bladimer Lopez, who slept by the Dumpster at a McDonald's on 125th Street, is in a supervised S.R.O. for the mentally ill run by the Center for Urban Community Services. So is Robert Whynot, who used to beg on the subways until he made $35, then bought himself a bag of heroin, half a gram of coke and a metro card ("so I wouldn't get arrested for fare-beating"). Now for the first time, at 40, he is getting treated for manic depression.

Even the New York City shelter system has made considerable progress, converting 1,000 shelter beds to mental-health-service beds run by nonprofits. These community programs cost between $10,000 and $43,000 per person, per year. All, however, are cheaper than a year at a state hospital ($135,000) or Rikers Island ($69,000).

The Push to Discharge

In 15 years of reporting on mental health, I have never seen the system in such disarray. Unprecedented cost-cutting measures are undermining safety valves that had long been in place. I count six dangers—for the mentally ill and the public—that have come into play in the last few years.

Danger 1: The last 6,000 long-term hospital patients that the state is working so hard to discharge are twice as likely to have a criminal background as patients from a decade ago.

Danger 2: While many of these patients could live in 24-hour supervised community residences, those beds are full. . . .

Danger 3: Psychiatric wards of general hospitals used to have the flexibility to keep a patient like Goldstein for months or transfer him to a state hospital for long-term care. But state hospitals are now taking few admissions, and managed care is pressing the general hospitals to discharge within three weeks. The five acute-care hospitals that treated Goldstein can receive up to $700 a day during those first weeks. But after that the medicated schizophrenic is usually considered "stable" by insurance monitors, and compensation can drop to $175 a day or be denied altogether. And even at $175 per day, hospitals lose money. As a result, there is a revolving door for patients, who quickly relapse without community support.

Danger 4: There are a record number of mentally ill in prisons and jails now being released—without any discharge planning.

Danger 5: The crackdown on Federal disability and welfare benefits will leave more mentally ill people with no Government support.

Danger 6: Government watchdog agencies like the Commission on Quality Care for the Mentally Disabled in New York have had their budgets cut and their jurisdictions narrowed in recent years. Over the last decade, the commission's staff has been reduced 25 percent. It is far less likely today to undertake major inquiries. During Gov. Mario Cuomo's administration, the Legislature authorized the commission to do a sweeping investigation of the adult-home industry; that authorization has not been renewed. . . .

The Latest Shortcut

For years, instead of resources, there have been shortcut solutions that push the problem around. The latest, inspired by the Goldstein case, is an effort to pass an outpatient commitment law for New York. It would allow people resistant to treatment to be committed to a supervised community program, and if they are not compliant with medication, they would be hospitalized. Supporters see it as a way to control the resistant mentally ill and leverage the system for more resources; if more people are committed to community programs, the state will have to build more. Opponents fear it will deprive the mentally ill of the right to control their treatment.

I doubt it would make much difference either way. The reality is that commitment is no longer much of a civil liberties threat—state hospitals don't want patients, and the short-term hospitals can't get

personal-property holdings desk and eventually it reverts to the U.S. Treasury. No matter how many times it happens, police soon find him again in the same restricted zone with several grand in his pockets.

A Scary Place

The police patrolling Lafayette Park who tell such stories do so with a wary look. So many strangers drift through this beat—tourists, protesters . . . and those separated from reality. The stories reflect frustration, humor, compassion and a bit of something else. "This is a scary place," one officer says. Find someone who has come to Washington to carry out a vendetta against a public official, and odds are that person has been in the park.

Some come for a day, some for nights on end. A handful are like nuclear protesters Ellen and William Thomas, who are not homeless but go home at night to a commune with an office and technology to support their antinuclear World Wide Web site. They have kept vigil for almost 18 years. But for the most part, every season the faces are new.

Another officer explains, "You don't know who they are or what they're doing until it's done." Also, he says, the street people of Lafayette Park have "strong convictions."

Yad B. Fantu, age 55, for example, came from Nigeria to warn the American public that President Clinton, House Speaker Newt Gingrich and Microsoft founder Bill Gates are "cutting babies' throats in the White House." He claims that the head of the FBI has tried to silence him, but he is immortal. ("You know that agent who killed himself in 1994? He was trying to shoot me, but the bullet bounced off my skin and killed him.")

The Communist

Nearby is Dwight, a handsome, gray-haired, 47-year-old in a ratty leather flight jacket. Another Lafayette Park regular, he came to Washington about 10 years ago to protest what he calls the "Secret Classified Gestapo." As a "communist opposed to the system," he objects to chemical preservatives and red dye, which he says the government is putting in "all foods at about 100,000 times the legal amounts."

Dwight says he was a husband and father working in real estate in Indianapolis when he became aware that he had been under "surveillance-harassment" since high school because his ancestors were communists. At that time, his family "became hostile," encouraging him to get treatment, so he knows they are aligned with government officials. "They, like everyone else, lie about it. They think it's nonsense, some sort of political dream. They think I'm paranoid, but I'm not. See me? I'm living on the streets. No one does that for a long time unless they have to."

He claims it's hard to be a communist in Lafayette Park. He gets attacked or arrested many times a year and says he will seek political asylum in Russia. "I hate the American people. I hate Americanism. I hate the people that believe all this," he says. "You go nuts out here after awhile."

Protecting People and Rights

In the meantime, the police do their job, which includes everything from protecting the street people and the public from interfering with each other to awakening the bench sleepers in the mornings to make sure they are not sick or dead. And these people know their rights: "It's a public park and I am the public. So let me be," is a common refrain.

The police are committed to upholding those rights unless—as the language of the law puts it—the street people show themselves to be a "danger to themselves or others." It is in defining this "danger" that conflict arises. "It's not against the law to have mental problems; it's not against the law to be homeless. You've got to remember that," says one officer. "We're not trying to get them locked up."

But when people are freezing because they can't be convinced to wear more than shorts in subzero weather, or when they show violent tendencies the officers believe could lead to a tragedy, detaining them overnight on mercy charges seems grossly inadequate. The officers often wish some of those they must watch would commit some offense serious enough to warrant a longer incarceration and a psychological evaluation—which might help them find a way out of the maze.

Scientific advances in diagnosis and treatment have helped many mentally ill people. And many services ranging from soup kitchens to literacy programs are available. But those whose minds are too crippled even to recognize that they are ill are "protected" by current laws from receiving help against their will. Some civil-liberties groups say that is how it should be—that involuntary treatment would deny the mentally ill their human rights. Others say that when patients are so ill they can't recognize their own condition, the only way to preserve their human rights may be carefully to mandate their treatment.

It is a public-policy issue, but it cannot be decided apart from its social and humanitarian context. Roughly one-third of America's homeless are like Weston—suffering from mental illnesses such as schizophrenia and manic depression. While the recent shootings have inflamed public perception, advocates of both the homeless and the mentally ill say neither group inherently is dangerous. Experts claim that only about 5 percent of the mentally ill exhibit violent behavior and then usually in cases in which treatment is rejected or not available. Those cases most often are among the homeless.

"They need so much in terms of connecting with the community," says Rutgers University professor Nancy Wolff, associate director of the Center for Research on the Organization and Financing of Care for the Severely Mentally Ill. Beyond a stable residence, such people need accountability and interaction. For this to occur, law-enforcement and mental-health officials must establish clear lines of communication.

As things stand now, police officers, charged with defending public health and safety, will pick up an offender and transport him to the hospital. The hospitals will cite civil-commitment laws that require evidence of being a danger to self or others, very narrowly defined. So law-enforcement officials find it easier to incarcerate than to commit.

"Our jails, whether we like it or not, are becoming our largest mental-health facilities," says Wolff. "D.C.'s [law enforcement] has an extraordinarily good mental-health-services program. Unfortunately, once they are released from the jail, they are without their medications."

Legal Reforms

The courts now occupy the border between medicine and law. Some mental-health courts are using a therapeutic rather than a punitive jurisprudence. They create "preconditional release arrangements" restoring defendants to the community on the condition that they receive treatment and stay on their medication.

It's a new mechanism, Wolff says, and still needs closer examination in terms of legal, clinical and social-welfare consequences. "We put the seriously mentally ill in the community because we believe they are full citizens, but we also need to expect them to live within the social norms and the laws of our system."

E. Fuller Torrey, president of the Treatment Advocacy Center in Arlington, Va., says that the same involuntarily enforced protective measures should apply to schizophrenics and manic depressives as to patients with Alzheimer's disease. "Why allow them to put themselves in very dangerous situations? We rationalize that as defending their civil liberties."

The laws are interpreted too narrowly, says Torrey, who believes intervention should be more common. It has come to the point, he says caustically, where "'dangerous to self' means committing suicide in front of your psychiatrists and 'dangerous to others' means trying to kill your psychiatrist." Torrey says the untreated mentally ill commit 1,000 homicides every year that could be prevented if involuntary treatment and commitment were allowed.

The need for a more cost-effective approach to treatment is acknowledged across the board: The average per-patient annual cost for managed care to the mentally ill is $70,000. Costs in the district exceed $100,000 per year.

Amador, the schizophrenia expert, says one key to resolving the dilemma between laws that are so broad that they easily can be abused and so narrow that they leave whole segments of the population without hope is to dispel some of the myths surrounding modern psychology. "It is pure myth that a person can fake psychosis or manipulate the system in such a way to make others believe that somebody has a psychotic disorder when they don't." Also, new drugs have less severe side effects than commonly is believed, and minimum effective dosages are prescribed.

Many mental-health professionals say that what is responsible for foot-dragging by policymakers is a combination of justifiable love of liberty and unjustifiable ignorance. "Lawmakers, lawyers and judges in the system need to be brought up to date," Amador says.

For now, the famous buttoned-down craziness of Washington's lawmakers is rivaled by the stories of the people in the shadows—dangerous or not—driven like the tragic Don Quixote to attack the windmills that are but voices in their minds.

ual must have a finger on the trigger of a gun before any medical care will be prescribed.

Utilizing Assisted Treatment Laws

Studies have proved that outpatient commitment [mandatory use of medication] is effective in ensuring treatment compliance. While many states have some form of assisted treatment on the books, the challenge remains in getting them to utilize what is at their disposal rather than tolerating the revolving-door syndrome of hospital admissions, readmissions, abandonment to the streets and incarceration that engulfs those not receiving treatment.

Adequate care in psychiatric facilities also must be available. Between 5 and 10 percent of the 3.5 million people suffering from schizophrenia and manic-depressive illness require long-term hospitalization—which means hospitalization in state psychiatric hospitals. This critical need is not being met, since we have lost effectively 93 percent of our state psychiatric hospital beds since 1955.

It is time to recognize that feel-good mental health policies have caused grave suffering for those most ill and that real solutions must be developed. The lives of millions of Americans depend on it.

MENTAL HEALTH TREATMENT SHOULD NEVER BE INVOLUNTARY

Vicki Fox Wieselthier

Vicki Fox Wieselthier is a self-described "psychiatric survivor" (a former psychiatric patient who is critical of the mental health system) and founder of MadNation, an organization that advocates social justice and human rights in mental health treatment. Wieselthier strongly opposes any form of mandatory treatment for persons in the mental health system. Laws that allow people to be involuntarily hospitalized or forced to take medication violate their right to make choices about their treatment, she insists. Wieselthier concludes that mental health treatment should be entirely voluntary.

I am against the use of force by the mental health system. Let me tell you why.

Force doesn't work. Well, that's not absolutely true. Force works very well if the goal is to keep people locked up and out of sight. Our society has given the state police powers to deal with folks that commit crimes or engage in activities that threaten our collective sense of well being. Increasingly force is used to lock up people with psychiatric labels just in case we might do something dangerous in the future. In many of our states, the fact that you have been locked up in the past gives the state the right to lock you up any time you miss a doctor's appointment, decide to stop taking medication that makes you feel like a zombie, or fight with your parents. Force may not make anyone "well", but it does get people out of the way. So in one sense it does work—just not for person who is the recipient of the force.

Force breeds more force. A variety of well-respected studies have shown that previous experience with force is the single most important factor influencing people who avoid seeking voluntary mental health care. People who have been locked up and forcibly drugged will go to almost any lengths to avoid contact with mental health professionals. And that leads to—yup—more forced treatment.

Force creates homelessness. The reason so many people are homeless is because there is a lack of safe, decent and affordable housing.

Reprinted from "If It Isn't Voluntary, It Isn't Treatment," by Vicki Fox Wieselthier, *Mad Nation,* 1998. Reprinted with permission from the author.

People diagnosed with mental illness are at increased risk for home-lessness because they are so often poor. Try paying for mental health care for awhile and you too can be poor. Poor people with mental ill-nesses are having an increasingly hard time finding housing that is not linked to receiving mental health care they neither want nor need. We all know that some people who are homeless avoid using emergency shelters because they are often dangerous places to be. HUD [Department of Housing and Urban Development] housing is also dangerous—or at least it can be if you have to take medicine you do not want and receive mental health care you do not need in order to stay housed. For far too many people the choice comes down to housing or freedom from psychiatric oppression.

The Costs of Force

Force is expensive. In the fall of 1997, the State of Illinois spent over ½ million dollars trying to drag Shirley Allen into a psychiatric hospital against her will. Ms. Allen was finally forcibly removed from her home. She spent a month in a hospital—refusing mental health care while she was there—and was released when the state finally admitted that she was neither incompetent nor dangerous. The State could have fed, educated, and housed a lot of poor people with the money they spent trying to drag Shirley off to the mental hospital against her will. Ironically, Shirley Allen may lose her home if she cannot come up with the money to pay for her forced incarceration.

Every dollar that is spent on force is a dollar that is not available to pay for alternative community based mental health care. The more force we pay for, the less we have to invest in things that really work—peer support, jobs programs, voluntary treatment.

Force kills. In Virginia, Gloria Huntley died after a month in which she lay strapped spread-eagled to a bed for 300 hours, including two stretches of 4½ days straight. Almost a year before Ms. Huntley died, her physician and psychiatrist wrote a memo warning Central State officials that Ms. Huntley would be more likely to die in restraints because she had asthma and epileptic seizures. The liberal use of restraints was part of Ms. Huntley's behavioral treatment plan, which meant it was supposed to have a therapeutic effect. In June of 1997, the Justice Department blamed Ms. Huntley's death on the punitive use of restraints.

Thousands of people diagnosed with mental illnesses kill them-selves each year. How many of them do you suppose kill themselves because they are unwilling to get involved in a system that uses force?

But you ask, don't we need force to control violent crazed killers? Sure do, but not forced psychiatric treatment (which is, after all, what we are talking about). That's why we have jails and the police. People who commit crimes should be prosecuted in the criminal justice system. Because we live in a humane society, we should have a humane penal system and people who are incompetent should be protected from harm in that system. People should be in the psychiatric system only when they have chosen to be there—just as people with heart disease are in the "cardiology system" only when they choose to be there. I say, if it isn't voluntary, it isn't treatment.

THE MENTALLY ILL ARE NOT MORE PRONE TO VIOLENCE

MacArthur Research Network on Mental Health and the Law

The MacArthur Research Network on Mental Health and the Law was created by the John D. and Catherine T. MacArthur Foundation to conduct research relevant to America's mental health laws. The following selection presents findings from the Network's research on the risk of violence committed by the mentally ill. According to the Network, the results of the research reveal that persons who have a mental illness, including schizophrenia, are no more likely to be violent than other people in the community unless they also have a substance abuse problem.

The risk that a person with mental disorder may physically harm others is a critical concern of both civil and criminal mental health law in the United States and in many other countries. On the civil side, involuntary mental hospitalization—and, increasingly, involuntary treatment and intensive supervision in the community—is often predicated on a clinical judgment of "dangerousness to others." In criminal law, involuntary treatment in a forensic hospital—and, also increasingly, involuntary community treatment and monitoring—for mentally disordered offenders turns on an assessment of undue risk of violence. Tort liability for clinicians who negligently assess risk, or who fail to take professionally appropriate actions to prevent assessed risk from being realized, has been the law in some American jurisdictions for 20 years.

Yet, despite legal mandates that violence risk assessments be routinely performed, a great deal of research conducted over the past 25 years suggests that the validity of such assessments is—at best—only modestly greater than chance.

The MacArthur Violence Risk Assessment Study

The MacArthur Violence Risk Assessment Study was designed with three purposes in mind: to improve the validity of clinical risk assessment, to enhance the effectiveness of clinical risk management, and to provide information on mental disorder and violence useful in reforming mental health law and policy.

Reprinted, with permission from The John D. and Catherine T. MacArthur Foundation, from the Executive Summary of *The MacArthur Violence Risk Assessment Study* published by the MacArthur Research Network on Mental Health and the Law at www.macarthur.virginia.edu/risk.html.

The risk factors studied in the research were culled from available "mid-range" theories of violence and of mental disorder, from our own clinical experience, and from those robust findings that have emerged from existing research by ourselves and others. These risk factors—some stable and some dynamic—were subsumed in four "domains": dispositional or personal factors, historical or developmental factors, contextual or situational factors, and clinical or symptom factors.

We used multiple measures to estimate the occurrence of violence to others in the community. The measures were patient's self-report, the report of a "collateral" (usually a family member), arrest records, and mental hospital records. The patient and collateral interviews took place five times over the course of the first year after the patient's hospital release (i.e., approximately every 10 weeks). We counted as "violent" a variety of aggressive acts that resulted in physical injury or sexual assault, or that involved weapon use or a threat that was made while the patient had a weapon in his or her hand.

A broadly representative sample of acute psychiatric admissions was involved in this study: both males and females; with and without prior violence; admitted on a voluntary or an involuntary legal basis; of all diagnoses (except mental retardation); and of white, African American, or Hispanic ethnicity. Subjects were between 18 and 40 years of age, and all spoke English.

Research methods and instruments were synchronized over three acute inpatient sites: the Western Psychiatric Institute and Clinic in Pittsburgh, Pennsylvania (a University-based facility), the Worcester State Hospital and the University of Massachusetts Medical Center, in Worcester, Massachusetts (a state hospital and a University-based facility), and the Western Missouri Mental Health Center in Kansas City, Missouri (a public-sector mental health facility). The average patient length-of-stay in these facilities was approximately 2 weeks. For reasons of statistical power, a total sample size of approximately 1,000 patients was set. . . .

Risk Categories

In brief, we were able to classify approximately three-quarters of the patients we assessed into one of two risk categories. "High violence risk" patients were defined as being *at least twice as likely* as the average patient to commit a violent act within the first 20 weeks following hospital discharge. "Low violence risk" patients were defined as being *at most half as likely* as the average patient to commit a violent act within the first 20 weeks following hospital discharge. Since 18.7% of all patients committed at least one violent act during this period, this meant that high violence risk patients had at least a 37% likelihood of being violent and low violence risk patients had at most a 9% likelihood of being violent.

PEOPLE WITH SCHIZOPHRENIA ARE MORE PRONE TO VIOLENCE

Sally Satel and D.J. Jaffe

The MacArthur Foundation has published research findings on the low risk of violence posed by people with mental illnesses, including schizophrenia. In the following article, Sally Satel and D.J. Jaffe insist that this research is flawed. Moreover, despite various methodological limitations, Satel and Jaffe argue, the research proves the opposite of what the investigators claim: It reveals that the mentally ill, particularly those with schizophrenia, are more violence-prone than the general population. Satel is a psychiatrist in Washington, D.C., and a lecturer at the Yale University School of Medicine. Jaffe is the co-founder of the Treatment Advocacy Center, an organization that seeks to revise laws to make it easier to provide mandatory treatment to people with severe mental illnesses.

In May 1998, Raymond Cook went on trial for first-degree murder in the death four years before of Thomas J. Guinta, a police officer in Fall River, Massachusetts. The same day that Cook shot Guinta, he spared the life of a longtime neighbor because he mistook her for a movie star who had played opposite James Cagney.

The day before Easter, 26-year-old Keith Powell of Red Oak, North Carolina, showed up with a shotgun at his aunt Louise's birthday party and killed his grandfather and two uncles. Months earlier when he walked away from his group home, his mother knew that he had quit taking his medication, and she feared that the voices in his head would soon return. After the shootings, Powell committed suicide.

In the most spectacular recent case, Michael B. Laudor of Hastings-on-Hudson, New York, a brilliant Yale Law School graduate who seemed to have beaten back his mental illness (he was working on a screenplay based on his successful fight) allegedly stabbed his girlfriend to death. He too had stopped taking his medication, and his mother had become so alarmed that she asked police to check on him shortly before his girlfriend's body was found.

Cook, Powell, and Laudor all suffered from schizophrenia. Lacking adequate treatment, they became deranged and violent. Homicide, to be sure, is rare even among schizophrenics, and yet untreated psychosis is so intimately linked to aggression that mental hospitals routinely rely on locked wards and often use physical restraints to control patients until antipsychotic medications take effect.

The connection between certain types of severe mental illness and violence would seem to be a matter of common sense. But until the 1960s, when deinstitutionalization began in earnest, most of the severest cases were out of sight, helping people forget how volatile the psychotic can be. And in the 1970s a movement focused on reducing the stigma of mental illness, and hence downplaying the risk of violence, became better organized and more influential. Thus, the old common-sense view became increasingly controversial.

The MacArthur Study

Now a new study from the MacArthur Foundation says the notion that people with serious mental illnesses may be particularly prone to violence is little more than a stigmatizing myth. The study got wide play in the media—including front-page coverage in the *New York Times* and some sensational headlines—from the AP, "Mentally Ill Not Especially Violent" and from the *Washington Post*, "Are Former Mental Patients More Violent? If They Don't Abuse Drugs and Alcohol the Answer Is Generally No, Study Finds." It could have a major impact on the running debate over involuntary-treatment laws by providing ammunition to civil libertarians and advocates for the mentally ill who believe that ill people should be left to wallow in their psychosis, haunting the streets of our cities.

The MacArthur findings were published in the May 1998 issue of the prestigious *Archives of General Psychiatry*, under the title "Violence by People Discharged from Acute Psychiatric Inpatient Facilities and by Others in the Same Neighborhoods." The study does admit that drugs and alcohol increase violence in people with mental illness more than they do in the general population, but it concludes that, otherwise, these people are no more violent than anyone else.

This contradicts the findings of numerous studies over the last thirty years. For example, a study of three hundred patients discharged from California's Napa State Hospital between 1972 and 1975 showed they had an arrest rate for violent crimes ten times higher than the general population. A 1994 British study of schizophrenics in Camberwell found that they were four to five times more likely than their neighbors to be convicted on charges involving serious violence. How did the authors of the MacArthur Violence Risk Assessment Study, all prominent researchers, come to such a radically different conclusion?

First, they excluded many potentially violent people by the way they constructed their sample, such as persons who were currently in or recently released from a prison, jail, forensic hospital, or long-term psychiatric hospital. "We always teach medical students that past violence is the best predictor of future violence," says psychiatrist and schizophrenia researcher E. Fuller Torrey. "While purporting to study violence, the first thing the authors did was omit violent people from the study."

The researchers limited the study to patients in acute-care hospitals. Only one in ten patients stayed longer than thirty days with half of all patients successfully treated and released in under nine days. This largely eliminated anyone too sick to be stabilized acutely, again reducing the chance of including non-psychotic individuals. Among those asked to participate, 29 per cent refused; a disproportionate number were suffering from schizophrenia, the very disorder which, if untreated, is most likely to result in violence.

Second, by choosing a narrow, high-end definition of violence, the study left out many dangerous people. For example, the authors counted as violence only those acts which produced bodily harm. As the father of a woman with schizophrenia and a mean left hook summed it up, "If you're a good ducker, your relative is not considered violent." While most of us would consider setting fires and trashing rooms to be violent acts, the authors of the study did not.

Conversely, the authors chose to study the broad category of mental illness rather than the narrow category of psychosis. Since people suffering from depression rarely commit violence against others, including them in the pool studied skews the results. In fact, 40 per cent of the sample suffered from depression.

Third, the researchers selected a violence-prone control group, residents of poor, chaotic, drug-ridden sections of Pittsburgh (one of the three cities from which the study drew patients) that had higher crime rates than the city as a whole. Since many of the patients were discharged to this same neighborhood, the authors assumed that a higher level of patient violence, if discerned, would be due to their mental illness. But this likely minimized the violence differential between the patients and the control group. That's because many people with psychiatric illnesses—illnesses that can impede economic advancement—end up living in marginal areas with hot-headed neighbors.

High Rates of Threatening Behavior

Despite all these stratagems, the authors still found that over half of the patients studied engaged in some form of threatening behavior within one year after discharge from the hospital. Specifically, 18 per cent of the patients without a drug or alcohol problem committed at least one act of violence (e.g., throwing objects, kicking, hitting, using a weapon) and an additional 33 per cent engaged in at least one act of aggression (same as above except that no harm resulted). Violence was nearly double (31 per cent) among mentally ill people who also abused drugs and alcohol.

So, in reality, the MacArthur study proves only that non-violent people tend to be non-violent. But the fact remains that seriously mentally ill people are more prone to violence than the rest of the population. Indeed, one of the MacArthur study authors acknowledges as much.

In a 1992 issue of *The American Psychologist,* John Monahan of the University of Virginia wrote: "The data that have recently become available, fairly read, suggest the one conclusion I did not want to reach: whether the sample is people who are selected for treatment as inmates or patients in institutions or people randomly chosen from the open community, and no matter how many social or demographic factors are statistically taken into account, there appears to be a relationship between mental disorder and violent behavior."

Stronger Laws Are Needed

Advocates will seize upon the MacArthur study as "proof" that all the other research is wrong—and that involuntary-treatment laws are unnecessary. In fact, those laws need to be strengthened, not repealed. Many states still rely solely on the standard of whether a person is "imminently and provably" dangerous to himself or others. What about those who are not yet dangerous but, already prisoners of their delusions, are likely to deteriorate further if not treated soon? A number of states allow the authorities to hospitalize such people against their will, but judges are notoriously reluctant to do so.

And many states do not allow judges to consider past violence when deciding whether someone should be committed. Even a court order for hospitalization does not guarantee medication, since in some states judges may not mandate that a hospitalized psychotic patient take an antipsychotic drug merely because he is dangerous: he must also be judged incompetent to refuse the medication. While over half the states permit judges to order a patient to continue to take his medication once he is discharged from the hospital (if he has a known habit of stopping the medication and becoming dangerous), such laws are actually applied only infrequently.

Obviously, treatment is of profound importance. It can keep people with serious mental disorders out of jails and shelters. It can prevent suicide and help the afflicted rejoin society. And certainty that the mentally ill will be treated might make communities less resistant to supervised housing and other desperately needed community-based programs. Yet, political correctness—an unwillingness to offend or "stigmatize"—prompts efforts to conceal the risk of violence from people suffering from unmedicated psychosis.

After years of denying the association between untreated mental illness and aggression, the National Alliance for the Mentally Ill, the largest and most influential grass-roots organization of family members of mentally ill people, has come full circle. Carla Jacobs, a NAMI board member from California, became an activist for involuntary commitment after her mother-in-law was fatally stabbed and shot by a mentally ill relative.

"We used to think it was stigmatizing to acknowledge violence," she says. "Now we recognize that violence by the minority tars the majority, and makes communities less likely to welcome the community-based housing that can facilitate treatment and reduce violence." Besides, she adds, "too many of our relatives are hurting others, and winding up in jail. The first step to helping them is admitting there's a problem."

Unfortunately, the MacArthur study will make it harder even to take that first, basic step.

CHAPTER 5

PERSONAL PERSPECTIVES ON SCHIZOPHRENIA

LIVING WITH SCHIZOPHRENIA

Stuart Emmons

The following selection is excerpted from Stuart Emmons's account of his struggle to live with delusions and perceptual distortions brought on by schizophrenia. In graduate school, he explains, he began to fear that people were trying to poison him. Later, while working as a teacher, Emmons became convinced that the school he worked for was "playing a game" with him. As a result of these symptoms, he was in and out of four hospitals between 1965 and 1969. Emmons is a poet and coauthor of *Living with Schizophrenia.*

In the winter of 1965, having graduated from August College *cum laude*, I began doing graduate work at Green University near Detroit. I had signed up for six courses of graduate work and was prepared, I thought, for a successful semester that would lead to a career in community college teaching.

My mother and father put a second mortgage on our family home in Lake City, Michigan, to provide the money for college. I was sure that within a year I would be teaching in a community college and be paying back the loan.

When my parents drove me to campus, I was scared. This was to be my first time away from them. They parked the car in front of Jason Hall, an older three-story brick structure. I found my room on the third floor. This was a time when colleges were overloaded with students. To my amazement, my two-man room would be home for three students. . . .

The room contained one large desk with a chair and drawers on each side. Two chairs for three students! The bedroom had three beds, two of which were bunk beds. Being the nice guy, I agreed to take the upper bed, and I even let my roommates have the bedroom window open when it was snowing out. I became terribly sick and slept with my clothes on and got better in 24 hours. One of my roommates got pneumonia.

I was very busy though I was happy. I studied until 11:00 every night. I liked going to a little restaurant for coffee in the morning, but other than that I didn't waste much time. On weekends, one of my dorm mates took me in his car to a nearby city for lunch. Occasionally, we went out with another graduate student, Steve Dunn.

I learned that there was a vacant room in Jason Hall, Room 13. I applied for and soon received it. I asked my roommates to help me move my possessions, but they said they were busy. So I moved my belongings as quickly as I could by myself. The room was a single, with a desk and bed in it, and I felt privileged to get it. It was a basement room next to a large dormitory study room. . . .

Strange Things

Strange things were beginning to happen. In the dining hall, a girl came up to me and asked me why, on the previous day, I had asked her not to sit next to me. I couldn't remember. And I had a strange desire to wear a red pullover shirt with a sport suit.

As the warmer weather of spring came, my room became very warm. Then I actually had bugs crawling on the floor, and I was horrified. The bugs multiplied rapidly and were on the floor day after day. I was becoming nervous and called a friend on the telephone. He suggested that I relax and listen to music on the radio. But I had loaned my radio to one of my former roommates, and I was convinced that he was listening to me on it. . . .

One night I was invited to listen to a foreign service official talk. I was suspicious of him and thought he thought I was a Communist spy. I didn't say anything. I just stared at him. . . .

One night I went to the shower room but found myself locked out of my room and I had forgotten the key. The next day I lost my key and had to get another one to get in my room. I was getting more and more nervous. I was asked if I forgot to bring the broom back to the office after cleaning my room. I thought they thought that I had stolen it. . . .

Fear of Poison

The bugs continued to crawl on the floor. I thought the Government was spying into my room with a telescope in a building across the street. I thought people in the cafeteria were loading my food down with salt. In criminology class, I thought the professor and the other students were laughing about me and directing the poisoning of my food in the cafeteria. I managed to live in spite of the poison. When I went to the cafeteria, my hand shook as the girl poured what I thought was poisonous coffee into my cup. I thought everyone in the cafeteria knew I was going to die. They all thought it was too bad, but I was so evil it was necessary. . . .

On a Saturday, I drank lemonade to try to neutralize the poison. Then I would take showers to try to sweat the poison out. I was so nervous I could hardly think. I thought I might only have hours left to live. I thought of taking a bus home to my parents. But no, it was too late for that. . . .

Saturday night I felt that there was an evil presence in my room on my bed. I dared not lie on the bed or I thought something terrible would happen. . . .

Appealing for Help

Then, that night, I did something incredible. With my thinking, I had an intellectual religion; I surrendered my intellect to Jesus. I opened the Bible and read "Be a fool for Christ." That was it, I thought. The only one I could appeal to was Jesus. That night I decided that I would see the administrative head of the dormitory the next day. I would tell him I thought that I was poisoned and wanted to see a doctor. I knew that if I was wrong, I would be considered mentally ill. But I couldn't lose. I would be a fool for Christ. . . .

Even in my paranoia—a word I would soon hear for the first time—I could trust Jesus. It was the turning point in my life. I was turning out from myself, out toward Jesus. I was making him my anchor when I thought I might die. Even in my confusion, I knew He was the only one who really understood me and knew what the truth was.

I knew Jesus was betrayed and knew what it was like when everyone seemed to be against Him. He would understand my situation. . . .

On Sunday morning, when I looked at a book, I wasn't even able to read. I went to the administrator of the dorm like I had planned. He had two graduate students walk me to the health center. A woman there gave me something to drink and, to my astonishment, I drank it. She offered to have me rest at her home a few days, but I declined. Then the two graduate students drove me a few miles to Grayling to the neuropsychiatric institute at Crown University.

In the Hospital

When I got there, a man in a white suit introduced himself as Dr. Black. I knew he was a psychiatrist but, because I could reason, I didn't consider myself insane. He asked me to sign in. I didn't want to, but I had no way to get back to the university that I was attending, so I did. Dr. Black left the room, leaving me alone for a short period. I heard voices coming from the heat vent. . . .

I thought that he put a speaker there to fool me. I was then led into a residence hall. I met people there who said "hello" but seemed lethargic. I told Dr. Black that they were just as sane as me. He said that was why I was there. I had always thought that insane people couldn't communicate. . . .

Soon I was in bed. I was offered a pill. I thought that if I took the pill offered me by the small nurse, I would die. But I was terribly tired, and I didn't feel like resisting my fate much longer. Finally, I took the pill, confident I would not wake up the next morning.

The next morning, to my astonishment, I awoke. I knew that I was not poisoned at Green University. I wanted to go back to my studies, but I was told that I must rest. I realized that I was paranoid, that I falsely thought that I had been persecuted. . . .

Now I was convinced that I was better and could not see why I had to be hospitalized. . . .

But I was still ill. I thought that Dr. Black had chosen his name so that I would realize that he was depressing. I thought that my room-mate, Eye Eagle, was a detective and that was why he called himself that. Actually, he was a very kind professor at Crown University who was suffering from the trauma of a recent divorce. Nobody seemed to be mentally ill to me. They were all just people with problems. . . .

One nice woman patient was a nurse who had been flown in. She told me she had spent a night with a patient who died and it had been too much for her.

It wasn't long before my dad came in. He looked like he had been crying. Still seriously mentally ill, I said, "Pa, I outdid Albert Einstein. I blew up my brains. He just developed the atom bomb." I thought that Dr. Black was listening to us. I thought he had the room bugged. . . .

It was not long before I knew most of the people on my floor of the building. There was the woman who had been in a car accident. There was the janitor too nervous to return to his job. There was the man with amnesia. There was a middle-aged heavyset woman who thought that she was dying from cancer. And there were the two high school students who had been on drugs. . . .

Signing Out

Then one day I realized I had signed in and I could sign out. I told Dr. Black that I wanted to sign out. He said I could, but that he'd like me to stay two more weeks. I signed out. In a few days, I would be home. I had stayed in the hospital four weeks. . . .

As he always liked to do, my father took the back highways going home instead of the freeways. It was an enjoyable ride home, and I noticed each high school as a possible place of employment. I wasn't planning to go back to Green University.

I went to the August College placement office, hoping to get a teaching job. They told me that there was an opening in Geral High School in Geral, Michigan, a farming community only eight miles or so southeast of Lake City. The job consisted of 11th-grade American history and 10th-grade English composition. I was delighted. I didn't admit on the application that I had been mentally ill. My dad said if I did, they wouldn't hire me. After I applied, I just relaxed, ready to enjoy the summer. . . .

In August, I received a call for a job interview with the Superinten-dent of the Geral schools. I dressed in my black suit and walked into the new high school building to the Superintendent's office. He hired me on the spot. It was 1965, and there was still a teachers shortage. I didn't realize then how fortunate I was, even when my dad said that my salary was more money than he had ever made in a year. . . .

The first year of teaching high school was a wonderful adventure. Compared to the effort I had put in each day in college, the work didn't seem hard at all. I taught three American history classes and two English classes. In American history, I had each class divided into committees, each committee having something to do with the teaching of the course. The busiest committee was the teaching committee. Its members directed the class by means of learning games. We had a wonderful time. I worked with a fine principal, superintendent, and faculty. In teaching English, I had my students work with the nature of words, then sentences, then paragraphs, and finally essays.

A Life-Shattering Experience

But on May 13, 1966, I had a life-shattering experience. The day before, my dad and I both had stayed home from work with bad colds. Dad and I talked and talked. That night I wanted to cook Dad a steak, but he said that he wasn't hungry. His lips looked blue. As he went to bed early, to my surprise, because he never went to church, he said that if I want to get married, I should go to church. The next day I went to school while Mom, also a teacher, stayed home from school to help Dad. That afternoon I had to stay late at school since it was my turn to proctor misbehaving students who had to stay after school. When I got home, I was shocked—Mom said Dad was in the hospital. I promptly drove Mom and me to the hospital. We went up to my father's room and found the door locked. A nurse came over and told us that my dad had died. He had had a breathing disease and died from heart failure. Our doctor gave my mother some strong tranquilizers to take. When we got back in my car to go home, I threw up. Mom and I were quiet with each other and comforted each other.

The next morning when I got up, the shock struck me again. Dad was gone! In the hospital, our doctor said I was now the man in the house and should take care of my mother. I took his words very seriously. My brother flew in for the funeral. He cried. My dad's mother who was still alive also came. She was gentle and kind to everyone. In a few days, I drove her home in the late afternoon, having to be prepared to teach the next morning. When I got back to the classroom, my work served as an antidote to what could have been a serious depression. I remember how comforting it was when students came up to me and said that they were sorry to hear that my dad died.

When summer came I was ready for fun. By submitting term papers, I completed three of the six courses I had taken at Green. I went to the beaches along Lake Michigan almost every day for a sun tan. I took Mom on lots of rides. . . .

Near the end of the summer, I got an apartment next to the movie theater on Lake City's main street. I didn't realize how cruel I was being to Mom by leaving her alone. It was a small apartment in a large grey house. My door led directly to the outdoors. I had one room for my kitchen and living room. I put my rock collection in the living room to divide it from the kitchen. I had a radio but no television.

Teaching Again

When my second year of teaching began, I sported a mustache and a nice new blue suit to go along with the rest of a very nice wardrobe. I had a deep tan and really felt fit. Now all five of my classes were 11th-grade American history. I had all the students I had the year before in 10th-grade English. Things seemed to be going really well. . . .

I was dating a very nice woman, the gym teacher. I took her to dinner at a beautiful restaurant on Dove Lake, to a movie in River Bend, to a high school football game, and to the high school home-coming. We had good times but I found I was starting to get exhausted easily. I couldn't seem to gain any weight even though I only weighed 125 pounds. . . .

Each day, I drove Jack, a crippled boy, to high school and back. I started saying strange things to him, such as that I believed the more money people spent, the more they would get. I also believed students and teachers were beginning to talk about me. . . .

When a government congressman talked to my class, I said I didn't like the way he used the word Government. He implied that I was a Communist when I said that nobody should be a millionaire. I thought no one should be worth that much. Eventually I thought that the entire high school was playing a game with me. One day in November, I had classes in the morning and parent-teacher confer-ences in the afternoon. In the first class that morning, I showed a movie dealing with the Monroe Doctrine. The President's Cabinet looked so serious in the film, I thought the film was a joke. Since I assumed that the film was made just to confuse me, I took the film and threw it in my wastebasket. Then I left school and drove to my apartment. I thought birds were following me. The sun seemed to be shining extra bright just for me. I thought that this was all in good fun, that the school system was just playing a game with me.

When I arrived at my apartment, the telephone rang and rang but I didn't answer it. It was all the game, and I thought I would play along. I drove my Mercury Comet out to Lake Michigan and walked along the beach. It was a marvelous November day. The sun was out, the sky was blue, and the waves pounding in along the beach seemed glorious.

Seka

After having completely relaxed, I drove to my mother's house, which seemed to have a strange perfumed odor. I put on a record of music written by a famous Finnish composer. It made me cry because it reminded me of a beautiful Finnish exchange student I had taught the year before, Seka. I loved her intensely. She was brilliant. She got a perfect score on one of my American history tests, the only student to do so. I didn't expect anybody to get a perfect score on my tests. They were meant to be a real challenge. I made them up myself and gave out As to students with less than perfect scores. As the day continued, my love for Seka grew. I came to think that at the end of the game people were playing with me, I would get to marry Seka. I believed that she was staying in town at my aunt's house and that she was being kept hidden from me. . . .

When I was in my apartment, I played the radio constantly. I thought all the radio programs were set up as part of the game. Songs were written, love songs, just for Seka and me—songs such as "There Is a Hush All over the World." That's how it began anyway. Once I thought I saw Seka way ahead of me on the main street of Lake City, just walking out of reach. I thought that eventually we would travel around the world as international citizens, ambassadors of good will. We would travel being carried by a huge balloon. . . .

One night I left my apartment and went to my mother's house. She was gone. I thought that she was with Seka. I took hundreds of slips of paper and wrote "Seka" on each one of them and put them all over the house to demonstrate how much I needed Seka. I cried and cried, I missed her so. I wrote poems dedicated to Seka, and I thought of the children we would have. She was in my thoughts every day. I continued to listen to the radio, thinking a code was being sent to me. I wrote all kinds of words for the code and came to the conclusion from what I wrote that my Dad was still alive and that he was part of the game too. I listened to Frank Sinatra sing "Shot down in April. . . ." My birthday was in April, so I thought that he was singing to me. The song went on, "I've been a prince, a pauper, a pawn and a king," and ended, "I think I'll roll up in a big ball and die." I thought that he was referring to the humor of the game. Another song that I thought referred to me was "Winchester Cathedral." . . .

I thought everyone was aware of me, including the people I saw downtown. When people opened their car doors, they were inviting me to get in. When they ate in restaurants, they pointed their silverware in ways that would get my attention. The lunch counter in a dime store vibrated for me.

Drawing and Driving

I drew pictures of the furniture in my mother's house, a fairly good one of the piano. I drew pictures of the furniture in the August College library. I mailed one of the pictures that I drew to an exchange student whom I had from Brazil the year before. (Then when I went in a grocery store the shelves seemed empty—for some reason only for me.) I drew pictures for my grandmother's birthday present, pictures of her furniture going back to when I was a child. It was such a light drawing that she could hardly see it. But she thanked me.

For a number of days, I took long fascinating drives in my car. I drove out past orchards along Lake Michigan. I was fascinated by the design of the trees. I thought that they were all especially constructed to be a new type of Disneyland. And all with me in mind. Once I drove quite a way north on a beautiful autumn day. A school bus went by full of kids, and I thought that they were all aware of me.

After a few weeks, I just stopped driving my car. (One day a man knocked on my door. I answered, and he had the keys to my car. He gave them to me and said I left them in the car and that somebody could have stolen it. I thanked him, but I thought no one would steal my car. People liked me too much to do that. The man must be part of the game. Besides, I thought, when the game was over, I would get the nice new Mercury Cougar parked at the Mercury-Lincoln dealership just down the street from my apartment.) . . .

My mother came to my apartment and I told her to go away. It was part of the game. My mother was always nice to me and laughing. I figured she knew about the game that was going on. She was wonderful. She was dating a nice guy, the janitor at her school. He was always happy too and knew about the game.

I thought my mom was having a wonderful time with the game. Besides, I had the illusion that a brilliant professor of philosophy I had at August College had been appointed as Mom's special comforter. He was a wonderful man, and I thought that he was seeing her and talking to her and just comforting her with his wisdom.

Wondrous Walks

I walked everywhere, no longer using my car. There was snow on the ground by December and it was cold. I looked at bare trees, and they looked unique and beautiful to me. Everything was beautiful. Everything contained God's love. When I looked at a tree, every part of it seemed to be something to marvel at. And the tree was itself connected to everything else, including the stars and the beautiful black spaces between them. And everything was connected ultimately to God. . . .

On cold, clear nights, the stars and space seemed to be filled with God's love. I wonder, wow, is this what Vincent Van Gogh was thinking of when he painted his famous "Starry Night"? . . .

All of my walks seemed wondrous. One night I walked on the August College campus. It was Christmas vacation, so I was the only one there. I walked into the Pine Grove, a lovely group of trees in the center of the campus. The trees cast big shadows on the thick snow in the moonlight. I came to the steps of Brown Hall where I had attended so many of my classes. I thought of just lying there and sleeping the night on the steps, but finally, I walked on. I walked past Central Park, the old town square. A few days later I wrote a poem about a ghost sailing ship anchoring above the park.

A Journey Through a Deranged World

Janice C. Jordan

In the following account, Janice C. Jordan describes her experience of becoming paranoid and delusional and hearing voices that told her what to do, think, and say. At one point, she recalls, her schizophrenia led her to believe the whole world could read her mind. Jordan explains that she was reluctant to tell others what was happening to her because she had difficulty trusting them and feared being labeled "crazy." Eventually she was helped by a good therapist and a psychiatrist who placed her on the new medication Clozaril. Jordan now works as a technical editor.

The schizophrenic experience can be a terrifying journey through a world of madness no one can understand, particularly the person traveling through it. It is a journey through a world that is deranged, empty, and devoid of anchors to reality. You feel very much alone. You find it easier to withdraw than cope with a reality that is incongruent with your fantasy world. You feel tormented by distorted perceptions. You cannot distinguish what is real from what is unreal. Schizophrenia affects all aspects of your life. Your thoughts race and you feel fragmented and so very alone with your "craziness."

My name is Janice Jordan. I am a person with schizophrenia. I am also a college graduate with 27 hours toward a master's degree. I have published three articles in national journals and hold a full-time position as a technical editor for a major engineering/technical documentation corporation.

I have suffered from this serious mental illness for over 25 years. In fact, I can't think of a time when I wasn't plagued with hallucinations, delusions, and paranoia. At times, I feel like the operator in my brain just doesn't get the message to the right people. It can be very confusing to have to deal with different people in my head. When I become fragmented in my thinking, I start to have my worst problems. I have been hospitalized because of this illness many times, sometimes for as long as 2 to 4 months.

Reprinted from "Schizophrenia: Adrift in an Anchorless Reality," by Janice C. Jordan, *Schizophrenia Bulletin*, vol. 21, no. 3, 1995, a publication of the National Institute of Mental Health.

I guess the moment I started recovering was when I asked for help in coping with the schizophrenia. For so long, I refused to accept that I had a serious mental illness. During my adolescence, I thought I was just strange. I was afraid all the time. I had my own fantasy world and spent many days lost in it.

The "Controller"

I had one particular friend. I called him the "Controller." He was my secret friend. He took on all of my bad feelings. He was the sum total of my negative feelings and my paranoia. I could see him and hear him, but no one else could.

The problems were compounded when I went off to college. Suddenly, the Controller started demanding all my time and energy. He would punish me if I did something he didn't like. He spent a lot of time yelling at me and making me feel wicked. I didn't know how to stop him from screaming at me and ruling my existence. It got to the point where I couldn't decipher reality from what the Controller was screaming. So I withdrew from society and reality. I couldn't tell anyone what was happening because I was so afraid of being labeled as "crazy." I didn't understand what was going on in my head. I really thought that other "normal" people had Controllers too.

While the Controller was his most evident, I was desperately trying to make it in society and through college to earn my degree. The Controller was preventing me from coping with even everyday events. I tried to hide this illness from everyone, particularly my family. How could I tell my family that I had this person inside my head, telling me what to do, think, and say?

However, my secret was slowly killing me. It was becoming more and more difficult to attend classes and understand the subject matter. I spent most of my time listening to the Controller and his demands. I really don't know how I made it through college, much less how I graduated cum laude. I think I made it on a wing and a prayer. Then, as I started graduate school, my thinking became more and more fragmented. One of my psychology professors insisted that I see a counselor at the college. Well, it appeared that I was more than he could handle, so I quit seeing him.

The Abyss of "Craziness"

Since my degree is in education, I got a job teaching third grade. That lasted about 3 months, and then I ended up in a psychiatric hospital for 4 months. I just wasn't functioning in the outside world. I was very delusional and paranoid, and I spent much of my time engrossed with my fantasy world and the Controller.

My first therapist tried to get me to open up, but I have to admit that I didn't trust her and couldn't tell her about the Controller. I was still so afraid of being labeled "crazy." I really thought that I had done something evil in my life and that was why I had this craziness in my head. I was deathly afraid that I would end up like my three paternal uncles, all of whom had committed suicide. I didn't trust anyone. I thought perhaps I had a special calling in life, something beyond normal. Even though the Controller spent most of the time yelling his demands, I think I felt blessed in some strange way. I felt above normal. I think I had the most difficulty accepting the fact that the Controller was only in my world and not in everyone else's world. I honestly thought that everyone could see and hear him. It progressed to where I thought the world could read my mind and that everything I imagined was being broadcast to the entire world. I would walk around paralyzed with fear that the hallucinations were real and the paranoia was evident to everyone.

My psychosis was present at all times. At one point, I would look at my coworkers and their faces would become distorted. Their teeth looked like fangs ready to devour me. Most of the time I couldn't trust myself to look at anyone for fear of being swallowed. I had no respite from the illness. Even when I tried to sleep, the demons would keep me awake, and at times I would roam the house searching for them. I was being consumed on all sides whether I was awake or asleep. I felt like I was being consumed by the demons. I couldn't understand what was happening to me. How could I convince the world that I wasn't ill, wasn't crazy? I couldn't even convince myself. I knew something was wrong, and I blamed myself. None of my siblings have this illness, so I believed I was the wicked one.

I felt like I was running around in circles, not going anywhere but down into the abyss of "craziness." I couldn't understand why I had been plagued with this illness. Why would God do this to me? Everyone around me was looking to blame someone or something. I blamed myself. I was sure it was my fault because I just knew I was wicked. I could see no other possibilities.

In the hospital, every test known to man was run on me. When the psychiatrist said I had paranoid schizophrenia, I didn't believe him. What did he know? He didn't know me. He was just guessing. I was certain he was trying to trick me into believing those lies. Nevertheless, he did start me on an antipsychotic medicine and that was the first of many drugs I have been given over the years.

This first medicine was Thorazine, the granddaddy of all psychoactive medicines. I have also, at one time or another, tried Mellaril, Stelazine, Haldol, Loxitane, Prolixin, and Serentil, to name a few. These medicines seemed to work for a while, but the symptoms always came back and the side effects were not pleasant. Many times, though, I began to think my medicine was poisoning me, and I would quit taking it. Then the "craziness" would return in full force. I would usually end up in the hospital and, with more medication, doctors would stabilize the psychosis. I tried to commit suicide twice during these periods. I wanted to punish myself for having this devastating illness. The Controller was trying to ruin my life. He was making me miserable. Yet I clung to him like a sinking ship, even though I felt like I was drowning, slowly but surely.

Getting Real Help

I was truly blessed when I started seeing my present therapist. I have been seeing him for the past 19 years. He has been the buoy in the raging waters of my mind. I was blessed again when I became the patient of my present psychiatrist. He has been taking care of me for over 16 years. They both have been my saviors. They have not hesitated to try new medicines and new approaches. No matter how bad things have been, they have always been there for me, pulling me back into the realm of sanity. They have saved my life more than once.

In fact, it was through them that I started taking Clozaril, a true miracle drug. It doesn't have half the side effects that the other neuroleptics have, and I have done remarkably well on this medication. The only problem with this medicine is its extremely high cost, which is why most people with schizophrenia are not taking it. Fortunately, my medical insurance covers the high cost of this drug. In fact, my medical insurance has paid for all of my hospitalizations and treatment. Sometimes I get scared that they will drop me, but I choose not to dwell on this fear.

I do know that I could not have made it as far as I have today without the love and support of my family, my therapists, and my friends. It was their faith in my ability to overcome this potentially devastating illness that carried me through this journey. There are so many people with serious mental illnesses. We need to know that we, too, can be active participants in society. We do have something to contribute to this world, if we are only given the opportunity. So many wonderful medications are now on the market, medications that allow us to be "normal." It is up to us, people with schizophrenia, to be patient and to be trusting. We must believe that tomorrow is another day, perhaps one day closer to fully understanding schizophrenia, to knowing its cause, and to finding a cure.

Thank you very much for listening to me. It is my hope that I have been one more voice in the darkness—a darkness with a candle glimmering faintly, yet undying.

CONFESSIONS OF A BAD PATIENT

Judi Chamberlin

Judi Chamberlin is a self-described "psychiatric survivor" (a person who has survived the mental health treatment system and now criticizes it from afar) and an activist for psychiatric patients. In the following selection, Chamberlin relates that when she resisted psychiatric treatment for schizophrenia, she was declared "non-compliant" and sent to a locked state hospital. There, she realized that in order to be released, she needed to pretend to be a "good patient." Outwardly she complied with treatment, Chamberlin writes, while inwardly she rebelled against the mental health system that she believed controlled the lives of patients and limited their chances of recovery.

A famous comedian once said, "I've been rich, and I've been poor, and believe me, rich is better." Well, I've been a good patient, and I've been a bad patient, and believe me, being a good patient helps to get you out of the hospital, but being a bad patient helps to get you back to real life.

Being a patient was the most devastating experience of my life. At a time when I was already fragile, already vulnerable, being labeled and treated only confirmed to me that I was worthless. It was clear that my thoughts, feelings, and opinions counted for little. I was presumed not to be able to take care of myself, not to be able to make decisions in my own best interest, and to need mental health professionals to run my life for me. For this total disregard of my wishes and feelings, I was expected to be appreciative and grateful. In fact, anything less was attacked as a further symptom of my illness, as one more indication that I truly needed more of the same.

I tried hard to be a good patient. I saw what happened to bad patients: they were the ones in the seclusion rooms, the ones who got sent to the worst wards, the ones who had been in the hospital for years, or who had come back again and again. I was determined not to be like them. So I gritted my teeth and told the staff what they wanted to hear. I told them I appreciated their help. I told them I was glad to be in the safe environment of the hospital. I said that I knew I was sick, and that I wanted to get better. In short, I lied. I didn't cry

Reprinted, by permission of the author, from "Confessions of a Noncompliant Patient," by Judi Chamberlin, *National Empowerment Center Newsletter,* 1999, www. power2u.org/recovery/confessions.html.

and scream and tell them that I hated them and their hospital and their drugs and their diagnoses, even though that was what I was really feeling. I'd learned where that kind of thing got me—that's how I ended up in the state hospital in the first place. I'd been a bad patient, and this was where it had gotten me. My diagnosis was chronic schizophrenia, my prognosis was that I'd spend my life going in and out of hospitals.

Learning to Hide the Outrage

I'd been so outraged during my first few hospitalizations, in the psychiatric ward of a large general hospital, and in a couple of supposedly prestigious private psychiatric hospitals. I hated the regimentation, the requirement that I take drugs that slowed my body and my mind, the lack of fresh air and exercise, the way we were followed everywhere. So I complained, I protested, I even tried running away. And where had it gotten me? Behind the thick walls and barred windows and locked doors of a "hospital" that was far more of a prison than the ones I'd been trying to escape from. The implicit message was clear: this was what happened to bad patients.

I learned to hide my feelings, especially negative ones. The very first day in the state hospital, I received a valuable piece of advice. Feeling frightened, abandoned, and alone, I started to cry in the day room. Another patient came and sat beside me, leaned over and whispered, "Don't do that. They'll think you're depressed." So I learned to cry only at night, in my bed, under the covers without making a sound.

My only aim during my two-month stay in the state hospital (probably the longest two months of my life) was to get out. If that meant being a good patient, if that meant playing the game, telling them what they wanted to hear, then so be it. At the same time, I was consumed with the clear conviction that there was something fundamentally wrong here. Who were these people that had taken such total control of our lives? Why were they the experts on what we should do, how we should live? Why was the ugliness, and even the brutality, of what was happening to us overlooked and ignored? Why had the world turned its back on us?

So I became a good patient outwardly, while inside I nurtured a secret rebellion that was no less real for being hidden. I used to imagine a future in which an army of former patients marched on the hospital, emptied it of patients and staff, and then burned all the buildings to the ground. In my fantasy, we joined hands and danced around this bonfire of oppression. You see, in my heart I was already a very, very bad patient!

The Right to Choose or Refuse Medication

One of the things I had already discovered in my journey through various hospitals, which culminated in my involuntary commitment to the state hospital, is that psychiatric drugs didn't help me. Every drug I was given made me feel worse, not better. They made me fat, lethargic, unable to think or to remember. When I could, I refused drugs. Before I got committed, I used to hide the pills in my cheek, and spit them out when I was alone. In the state hospital, I didn't dare to try this trick. I dutifully swallowed the pills, hating the way they made me feel, knowing that, once I was free, I would stop taking them. Once again, I was non-compliant in thought before I could be non-compliant in deed.

Now I want to make one thing very clear here. I am not advocating that no one should take psychiatric drugs. What I am saying, and I want to make sure this point is understood, is that each individual needs to discover for himself or herself whether or not the drugs are part of the solution or part of the problem. Many people I know and respect tell me that they would not be where they are in their recovery were it not for the particular drugs that they have found work for them. On the other hand, many others, of which I am one, have found that only when we clear ourselves of all psychiatric drugs do we begin to find the road to recovery. We need to respect these choices, and to understand that there is no one single path for all of us.

Psychiatric drugs, like all drugs, have side effects. If the positive effects outweigh the negative effects, then people will generally choose to take the drugs. When the negative effects, however, outweigh the positive ones, then the choice not to take the drugs is a good and reasonable one. Side effects can be more easily tolerated when one is gaining something positive in return. Let me give an example from my own experience. Every day, I take anti-inflammatory drugs to control the symptoms of arthritis. Without these drugs, I would be in pain much of the time, and find it difficult to move easily. I'm willing to put up with the danger of developing ulcers (and I take another drug to help protect my stomach), because the cost/benefit ratio works out in my favor. If, on the other hand, the anti-inflammatory drug didn't relieve the arthritis pain, then the cost/benefit ratio would go the other way, and I would stop taking the drug and discuss with my rheumatologist what other approach to try.

Here is the key difference between what happens to psychiatric patients and what happens to people with physical illnesses. With my rheumatologist and with my lung doctor (I also have a chronic lung disease), I am a full partner in my own treatment and recovery. I am consulted, listened to, and given the information I need to make informed choices. I acknowledge that the doctors have expertise that I lack, and they, in turn, acknowledge that I have information about the workings of my own body that they need to guide them in their recommendations. Sometimes we disagree. Then we talk about it. Sometimes I take their advice, while other times I don't.

Psychiatric patients, on the other hand, are usually assumed not to know what is best for us, and to need supervision and control. We are often assumed to be talking in code; only so-called "experts" can figure out what we really mean. A patient who refuses psychiatric drugs may have very good reasons—the risk of tardive dyskinesia [a disorder caused by psychiatric medication that produces involuntary movements of the mouth, limbs, and hips], for example, or the experience of too many undesirable negative effects. But professionals often assume that we are expressing a symbolic rebellion of some sort when we try to give a straightforward explanation of what we want and what we don't want. I'm sure you've all heard the many psychiatrist jokes that feature the punch line, "Hmm, I wonder what he means by that?" Well, doctor, I want to tell you, we usually mean just what we are saying. In the slogan of the women's movement: "What part of no don't you understand?"

Recovery for All

I consider myself a very lucky person. I don't think that I have some special talent or ability that has enabled me to recover when so many others seem stuck in eternal patienthood. I believe that recovery is for everyone. In the words of the mission statement of the National Empowerment Center, we carry a message of recovery, empowerment, hope and healing to people who have been diagnosed with mental illness. We carry that message with authority because we are a consumer-run organization and each of us is living a personal journey of recovery and empowerment. We are convinced that recovery and empowerment are not the privilege of a few exceptional leaders, but rather are possible for each person who has been diagnosed with a mental illness. Whether on the back ward of a state mental institution or working as an executive in a corporation, we want people who are mental health consumers to regain control over their lives and the resources that affect their lives.

One of the elements that makes recovery possible is the regaining of one's belief in oneself. Patients are constantly indoctrinated with the message, explicit or implicit, that we are defective human beings who shouldn't aim too high. In fact, there are diagnostic labels, including "grandiosity" and "lack of insight," to remind us that our dreams and hopes are often seen as barriers to recovery instead of one of its vital components.

Defining "Recovery"

Professionals and patients often have very different ideas of what the word "recovery" means. Recovery, to me, doesn't mean denying my problems or pretending that they don't exist. I have learned a lot from people with physical disabilities, who think of recovery not in terms, necessarily, of restoring lost function, but of finding ways to compensate or substitute for what one may be unable to do. Some of the most able people I know, in the true sense of the word, are activists in the physical disability movement—they may not be able to see, or hear, or move their limbs, but they have found ways to do the things they want to do despite these difficulties and despite those professionals who advised them not even to try. Without our dreams, without our hopes for the future, without our aspirations to move ahead, we become truly "hopeless cases."

I often hear professionals say that, while they support the ideas of recovery and empowerment in principle, it just won't work for their clients, who are too sick, too disabled, too unmotivated. Whenever I hear these objections, I want to know more about what kinds of programs these professionals work in and what goes on there. I know that the professionals who knew me as their patient thought the same things about me. That's the dilemma of the "good patient." A good patient is one who is compliant, who does what he or she is told, who doesn't make trouble, but who also doesn't ever really get better. A "good patient" is often someone who has given up hope and who has internalized the staff's very limited vision of his or her potential.

Now, again, I want to make myself clear. I'm not saying that mental health professionals are evil people who want to hold us all in the grip of permanent patienthood and who don't want us to get well. What I'm saying is that there's something about being a "good patient" that is—unintentionally, perhaps—incompatible with recovery and empowerment. When many of us who have become leaders in the consumer/survivor movement compare notes, we find that one of the factors we usually have in common is that we were labeled "bad patients." We were "uncooperative," we were "non-compliant," we were "manipulative," we "lacked insight." Often, we were the ones who were told we would never get better. I know I was! But twenty-five years of activism in the consumer/survivor movement has been the key element in my own process of recovery.

A Limited View of Patients' Abilities

Let's look at this word "compliance." My dictionary tells me it means "acquiescent," "submissive," "yielding." Emotionally healthy people are supposed to be strong and assertive. It's slaves and subjects who must be compliant. Yet compliance is often a high value in professionals' assessments of how well we are doing. Being a good patient becomes more important than getting well. It's like the healthy woman/healthy person dilemma. Psychological researchers have found that while emotionally healthy adults, gender unspecified, are supposed to be assertive and ambitious, emotionally healthy women are supposed to put others' needs before their own. If you're a woman and fulfill the stereotyped "woman's role," then you're not an emotionally healthy person. If, on the other hand, you are strong and assertive, then you can be labeled as not being an emotionally healthy woman.

Getting better, we were informed by staff, meant following their visions of our lives, not our own. Let me give you an example, from a book called *Reality Police* by Anthony Brandt:

> [Brandt says] I was thought to be a hopeful case, for example, so the doctor assigned to it worked up a life plan for me. . . . I was to stay in the hospital three months or so to stabilize my life, she said. When I seemed up to it, I would go to work in the hospital's "sheltered workshop" where I would make boxes for IBM and be paid on a piecework basis. When I had made enough boxes I would then be moved to the halfway house in Kingston, across the Hudson, where they would arrange a job for me in a special place called Gateway Industries established for the rehabilitation of mental patients. There I would pre-sumably make more boxes. Eventually I might move out of the halfway house into my own apartment.

What Anthony Brandt's doctor didn't know was that Brandt was not a "mental patient" at all. He was a writer who had feigned the symptoms of mental illness in order to find out first hand what the life of a mental patient was like. He had a successful career and a real life that he could return to. He didn't have to accept a limited view of his abilities and potential. Most real mental patients are not so lucky.

Encourage People to Dream

Anthony Brandt wrote his book in the mid '70's, but what happened to him unfortunately continues to happen today. All those "unmoti-vated clients" I keep hearing about are the ones who are on a silent sit-down strike about others' visions of what their lives should be like. When I ask professionals what it is that their clients are "unmotivated" about, it usually turns out to be washing floors or dishes, on the one hand, or going to meaningless meetings on the other. Would you be "motivated" to reveal your deepest secrets to a stranger, for example, someone you have no reason to believe you can trust with this sensi-tive information? And, more important, should you be "motivated" to do so? People, in general, are motivated to do things that they want to do or which will get them things which they want. Just because someone has a diagnosis of "mental illness" doesn't change that fundamental fact of human nature. All the time and energy that mental health professionals seem to put into "motivating" their clients to do things they don't want to do would, I think, be better spent helping clients to figure out what things they want for them-selves and the strategies to achieve them.

We need to start encouraging people to dream, and to articulate their own visions of their own futures. We may not achieve all our dreams, but hoping and wishing are food for the human spirit. We, all of us, need real goals to aspire to, goals that we determine, aims that are individual and personal. I feel crushed when I visit programs that are training their clients for futures as residents of halfway houses and part-time workers in menial jobs. And if I, a visitor, feel my spirit being crushed, how do the people trapped in those programs feel?

Researchers have asked clinicians what kinds of housing, for example, their clients need, and have been told that congregate, segregated housing was the best setting. At the same time, the researchers have asked the clients directly what kind of housing they want, and have been told that people would choose (if they were given the choice) to live in their own homes or apartments, alone, or with one other person they had chosen to live with. At the end of the year, the researchers found, the clients who got the kind of housing they wanted were doing better than the clients that got the housing that was thought to be clinically appropriate. Helping people to reach their goals is, among other things, therapeutic.

Celebrating the Spirit of Non-Compliance

One of the reasons I believe I was able to escape the role of chronic patient that had been predicted for me was that I was able to leave the surveillance and control of the mental health system when I left the state hospital. Today, that's called "falling through the cracks." While I agree that it's important to help people avoid hunger and homelessness, such help must not come at too high a price. Help that comes with unwanted strings—"We'll give you housing if you take medication," "We'll sign your SSI [Social Security Income] papers if you go to the day program"—is help that is paid for in imprisoned spirits and stifled dreams. We should not be surprised that some people won't sell their souls so cheaply.

Let us celebrate the spirit of non-compliance that is the self struggling to survive. Let us celebrate the unbowed head, the heart that still dreams, the voice that refuses to be silent. I wish I could show you the picture that hangs on my office wall, which inspires me every day, a drawing by Tanya Temkin, a wonderful artist and psychiatric survivor activist. In a gloomy and barred room a group of women sit slumped in defeat, dressed in rags, while on the opposite wall their shadows, upright, with raised arms and wild hair and clenched fists, dance the triumphant dance of the spirit that will not die.

A Teenager's First Psychotic Episode

Pamela Grim

Pamela Grim is an emergency room physician and the author of *Just Here Trying to Save a Few Lives: Tales of Life and Death from the ER*. In the following article, she describes her treatment of a seventeen-year-old boy who was brought to the emergency room due to his strange behavior, including attempting to restart his dead hamster's heart with a car battery. Grim recalls explaining to the boy's parents that he was likely having his first "psychotic break," or his first departure from a normal orientation to reality. Her account illustrates the difficulty that parents of people with schizophrenia have in understanding and accepting that their formerly healthy child may face a lifelong struggle with a debilitating disease.

"Wow, here's one for you." I looked up from the chart I was writing out. Two policemen stood before me, flanking a reedy young man, a kid really, dressed in shabby clothes. One of the officers lifted up a paper bag and shook it. "We got called by this kid's parents. They said he was acting goofy, high on drugs or something. We found him with this."

Bill, the emergency room charge nurse, peered over the top of his glasses. "Okay," he said. "What's this?"

"This," the officer said, shaking the bag again, "is a hamster—a dead hamster."

Bill pushed his glasses back in place, waiting for the payoff. "Uh-huh," he said.

The second officer leaned forward. "He had it in his mouth."

I hadn't been listening closely, but at this point I stopped working on my chart and looked up at the boy. Bill didn't even skip a beat. "Did he say why?"

Scarcely audible, the boy answered, "CPR."

"Yeah," Officer Number One added. "He told us that he was trying to perform CPR on the hamster. That's why he had it in his mouth."

"And he was doing this in the garage," said Officer Number Two. "He had the car hood up and the battery out of the car and he had—"

Excerpted from "Tough Love," by Pamela Grim, *Discover*, September 1996. Copyright © 1996 by Pamela Grim. Reprinted with permission from *Discover*.

"—He had some stereo wires hooked up to the battery and was trying to shock the hamster," Officer One broke in. "You know, defibrillate it—like the paramedics do. That's when his parents called us."

Bill looked directly at the boy. "You tried to defibrillate a hamster?"

The boy nodded and took a deep breath. "It seemed like a good idea."

Searching for Answers

His parents showed up half an hour later. I still hadn't had a chance to get in to see the boy. All I knew was that he was 17, older than he looked. His parents, the Deans, were well dressed, very well dressed. They must have come from a well-to-do neighborhood out of the usual service area of our ER. The father was wearing an expensive suit; the boy's mother—tall, slender, and elaborately coiffed—was carrying an expensive leather handbag. They glanced around nervously at the usual bad-news ER crowd. A woman sat next to them, holding some bloody gauze to her head. She was a prostitute who had suffered a scalp wound inflicted by her pimp. On the other side of them were gurneys, where drunks were sleeping it off.

I introduced myself to the Deans and took them over to a quiet corner. "So," I said, "what's been going on?"

"I think it's drugs," Mr. Dean said. "I don't know where he's getting them."

"Randall's never touched drugs," Mrs. Dean said vehemently. "I don't know how you can think that."

"How else do you explain all this?" Mr. Dean whispered fiercely to Mrs. Dean.

"I can't," Mrs. Dean replied, equally fiercely. "But there has to be an answer." She stood there tight-lipped, ashen-faced. Obviously these two had been disagreeing about their son for years. They looked off in different directions, both appearing anxious and bewildered.

"Tell me what the problems have been," I said.

Mrs. Dean groped for words. I could see she was not accustomed to sharing details from family life with a stranger, even if the stranger was a doctor. "Last week he got the keys out of my purse and went joyriding. He ended up smashing the car. I couldn't believe it. He knew he wasn't supposed to be driving the car."

"He's always been more or less of a discipline problem," Mr. Dean added. "Basically he's a good kid, but he's so damn irresponsible. We took him to see a psychologist last year, and the psychologist did all these tests and said he had . . . What is it he's supposed to have?"

"Attention deficit disorder," said Mrs. Dean.

"Right, attention deficit disorder. Which makes sense to me in a way. He can't finish anything he starts."

Mrs. Dean broke in. "The psychologist said he was learning disabled. Or dyslexic. She said this is why Randall does so poorly in school when he's so very bright according to his test scores."

"About the hamster," I said.

"He's a bright boy," Mr. Dean said. "He knows everything there is to know about taking a bicycle apart and putting it back together. He spends hours and hours in the garage."

"The hamster—" I said again.

"Rocky? Oh, he's had that old hamster for years." Mr. Dean sighed, still absorbed with his own worries about Randall. "He hasn't been attending classes at school all year. I'm sure he's going to flunk several courses."

"I guess we spoiled him," his mother added. "We never went through anything like this with our other children." Mrs. Dean paused and took a deep breath. "The school psychologist says that a big part of the problem is that Randall has absolutely no self-esteem."

Mr. Dean stared down at his hands. "How can you give your child everything and he still ends up with no self-esteem?"

"I understand," I said. I was lying. I was sure I didn't understand any more than they did.

"We've been desperate," Mrs. Dean said. "Nobody can give us any answers, so a couple of months ago we went to this seminar on Tough Love."

"I'm sorry," I said. "What?"

"Tough Love. It's a course on how to, well, set limits on your children." She reached into her handbag and took out a hardback book. The title said something about Tough Love and child rearing.

Violent Thoughts

At this point a patient came in with fluid in the lungs, so I rushed off and didn't get back to the Dean family for another hour. When I returned, the parents were sitting off to one side, arms folded stiffly, the mother with her purse in her lap. Randall sat on the examining table.

"Hi, Randall. I'm the ER doctor today."

The boy, looking down at his sneakers, said nothing.

"Randall," I said gently, "what was this about you stealing the car?"

Randall shrugged his shoulders, head down. "They wouldn't let me drive the car."

Mr. Dean broke in. "He lost his driving privileges because of his grades. When he brings his grades up, he can use the car."

"Randall," I said, "how do you feel about that?"

The boy looked up suddenly at his father. "I knew I wasn't supposed to drive it, but I was confused. I wrecked it."

"Randall," Mr. Dean said, leaning forward, "are you doing drugs?"

Randall thought for a moment, as if he were trying to remember.

"No, not for a while."

"Randall," I said, pulling my chair up close, "did you kill your hamster?"

The boy slowly nodded his head.

abnormalities ultimately cause severely disordered thinking.

Symptoms can wax and wane, but during a break, patients are often disorganized and delusional. Frequently they require hospitalization. At other times patients may be able to function more normally, but many can never live independently. Although recent advances in medication have allowed many schizophrenics to lead productive lives, most patients continue to have some symptoms of thought disorder. No one is ever cured.

A baby howled in a nearby room as I walked back to the nurses' station. I had a headache and, for some reason, this headache was associated with a mental image of Mr. and Mrs. Dean, not as they were now but as they appeared shortly after the birth of their last son, Randall. I could see proud parents and a sleeping baby. I could envision the big plans, high expectations, good schools, tennis lessons, piano recitals—all the things attentive parents lavish on their last child.

I sat down at the desk and put Randall's chart in front of me. "Seventeen-year-old male, previously healthy, presents with—" I stopped. Presents with what? Psychosis? Illusions? Hallucinations about the sewer system? A whole new and senseless world? I thought about Mr. and Mrs. Dean stumbling into this other world—a world of institutions, mind-numbing tranquilizers, locked wards, and disembodied voices.

For a moment I hated my job. Randall's parents may as well throw the Tough Love book out the window; their son's problems lie far beyond its reach. Maybe I'm wrong, though; I'm not a psychiatrist. Another image of Mr. and Mrs. Dean flickered through my mind. I could see them sitting in the dayroom of a psychiatric ward in some prestigious institution. They are dressed up for a visit with their son. They are nervous. After a while the room starts to fill with psychiatric patients, people whose paths the Deans never dreamed they would cross: street people, the homeless, the psychotic, the depressed, the muttering old women and the stiff-gaited young men, the manic addicts, the zombies. The Deans are sitting in this place, waiting for their son, holding each other's hands. It is here that they finally see that even if they give their son all the love in the world, it may still not be enough.

MY SON'S STRUGGLE WITH SCHIZOPHRENIA

Madeline Marget

Madeline Marget recounts the struggles of her son, Charlie, whose schizophrenia drove him to commit suicide at the age of twenty. Described by one psychiatrist as "too sensitive for this world," Marget writes, Charlie was plagued by fears and believed death would allow him to transcend to a "more interesting plane" involving time travel, mental telepathy, and spaceships. Charlie was also troubled by the negative symptoms of schizophrenia, including apathy and social withdrawal, she recalls. Marget is the author of *Life's Blood*, a book about the experience of bone marrow transplantation and treatment for blood disease (Simon and Schuster, 1992) and a frequent contributor to *Commonweal* magazine.

My son, Charlie, died in 1999 at 20.

Charlie was many things: kind, deeply intelligent, and sometimes hilariously witty. His hands were elegant, with long, slender fingers, and he moved them delicately, precisely. He had blue eyes and brown hair, a small nose, a full mouth, thick eyebrows. Charlie was 6-foot-4, upright and lean, with broad shoulders; beautiful to look at.

And, in his last months, he was increasingly frightened. He could not explain what, exactly, scared him.

A Little-Understood Disease

"Charlie died of a terminal disease," both his older sister and his twin sister said, independently, when I called to tell them he had died. They were right, of course. But schizophrenia is not like most diseases. Nor is it necessarily fatal.

Many people live with schizophrenia. Some never really improve, some "stabilize" (meaning their behavior becomes predictable), and some recover, becoming able to manage on their own. It is a broad diagnosis that, like cancer, manifests itself in many ways. Little is known about cause and cure. The word schizophrenia is too inclusive to be explanatory.

Reprinted from "Too Sensitive for This World," by Madeline Marget, *Boston Globe*, June 13, 1999.

One can make two plain statements about schizophrenia: It is a physical disease of the brain, and a person afflicted with it has a serious mental illness. Beyond that are maybes, unknowns, and misunderstandings. Charlie's life was no exception.

After our son's death, Jeff, a high school friend of Charlie whom we'd never met, wrote us a long, typed, single-spaced letter. He said Charlie—two years his senior—had been "a good mentor and a good friend." He said Charlie taught him how to play chess, how to throw a Frisbee, what a palindrome was. He changed Jeff's political views "by reasoning through my rhetoric and showing the flaws in my arguments."

And "Charlie was always genuine with me," wrote Jeff. "He never laughed at anything he didn't think funny and he always spoke his mind when asked for his opinion. As introverted as he was, Charlie was a leader; he led by example. I rarely heard him utter profanities; he was always kind to the janitors in our school. . . ."

At the time of which Jeff wrote, Charlie's illness had long since shown itself, though not everyone saw the symptoms and no one recognized it for what it was. The psychiatrist we sent him to the summer of his junior year, after he had threatened suicide, diagnosed Charlie as depressed over adolescent worries about girls and sex.

Signs of Trouble

In retrospect, however, clear signs of psychosis were present then. Charlie was extremely quick to anger, often with very little, or no, provocation. He became preoccupied with thoughts of death.

For a few months during the year Jeff met him, Charlie stopped going to school, although a loving teacher and caring school administrators managed to coax him back. He became increasingly volatile, but my husband, daughters, and I interpreted his strangeness as a variety of acceptable idiosyncrasy and took extra care not to upset him. All of us wanted to give him whatever of ourselves might help him to grow out of the difficulty we knew was there.

Charlie's difficulties had been evident—at least to me—almost from his birth. When he was just a few weeks old, Charlie didn't seem appropriately responsive. "A contemplative," declared a friend's mother, a woman who had raised five children, and I was glad to have a positive word to blot out my worry. Yet I knew there was something unusual in the way he screamed the moment I left a room, and stopped, as if a switch had been pulled, the minute I returned.

He was late to smile and walk and was wary of new situations, despite, especially during his early years, the companionship and support of his twin sister.

Through most of his school years, I asked Charlie's teachers if they had concerns about him. All but one reassured me that he was fine; the one who did not, a sixth-grade teacher infelicitous in her phrasing but correct in her thinking, said, "Something's wrong with that kid."

She had no suggestions except to "take him to someone, if you know someone good."

We didn't. Our previous experience with counseling had not been positive. When Charlie was 8, my sister was diagnosed with leukemia, and I donated bone marrow to her. During that time, Charlie grew terribly upset—throwing clothes around his room, erupting without obvious cause, saying he wished he were dead. But the psychologist to whom we took Charlie not only misdiagnosed him, but antagonized him. "Talk therapy," we later learned, is disruptive for psychotic people because it tears at an emotional fabric that is already unraveling.

Still, in these family sessions, my husband and I confessed our sins: I had raised my voice, Ernie had been preoccupied. We had never struck Charlie, we had never called him names, we praised him and loved him, but I, at least, was willing, even eager, to blame myself for his difficulties. If Charlie's problems were my fault, I could solve them.

Charlie's behavior became more peculiar. He seemed, in the words of one psychiatrist, "too sensitive for this world," even as he lived what—on the surface—seemed a relatively normal life. He finished high school, but grew unable to meet my gaze, and had trouble meeting anyone's. He went off to college, but when he came home to visit, he treated our house, his home, as if it were full of strangers. He carried his towel, toothbrush, toothpaste, and soap back and forth to the bathroom. He kept his laundry separate, and after family meals he washed his dishes but no one else's.

He slept in his clothes. And whenever possible—such as the last two summers of his life—he slept all day and was awake all night.

The nights, he explained, were more peaceful.

Suicide Attempt

At the beginning of his junior year of college, Charlie had a psychotic breakdown, and tried to kill himself.

We had known that his thoughts about death, present for a long time, had intensified, and the distortions in his thinking, on that subject especially, had grasped him more and more tightly. But we had not known how tightly.

Charlie spent over a month in a psychiatric hospital, said to be one of the best in the country. At the time of his admission, doctors told us he might kill himself even while he was there, locked up and constantly checked. He didn't, although his stay was torture for him.

Every day when I visited him he begged for release. He said he felt like an animal, locked up. It was the confinement that bothered him most, but the nature of the place was hard on him, too—things such as the hard beds and pillows designed, no doubt, to thwart suicide attempts. "I want a comfortable room," Charlie said, and to me it seemed little enough to ask—a place of ease to rest his body and head, with all its troubles.

Now, I go into his room and kiss the red corduroy bedspread that covers the comfortable pillow he had here at home. Though we washed his bedclothes after he died, the place where Charlie slept still smells like him, at least to me. It is evidence of his life, a life that should be continuing.

While Charlie was in the hospital, my husband and I first heard of a symptom of mental illness referred to as having "a tenuous sense of self." At first, I thought the phrase meant that Charlie didn't have a strong sense of his identity, which was in a way true. But tenuous sense of self is a far more extreme, a far stranger perception.

A person afflicted with a tenuous sense of self has lost, or never gained, the usual boundaries between himself and other people and objects. "Such a person's thoughts and emotions are not coordinated . . . the self isn't integrated," explained Stephen Jaffe, a psychiatrist we consulted about Charlie. He held out his hand and turned it slightly. "He might look at his hand and think, 'What am I doing here?' and 'What am I doing?'. . . There's a lack of inner cohesion. The sense of self is like 'Guernica.'" Imagine, in short, not looking at Picasso's painting, but being it.

Although Charlie never specifically described such perceptions to me, that world—fractured, frightened, isolated in confusion and torment—seemed to be his. In such a place, it doesn't seem possible that one would recognize his own condition. Charlie didn't.

The law where we live says an adult—anyone over 18—can be held against his will only if he is an imminent danger to himself or others; imminent is defined as within 48 hours. After five weeks, the doctors judged Charlie's long-term risk of suicide—or "lethality," as the doctors' cold jargon put it—to be high, but saw no imminent danger. One doctor also noted that confinement was bad for people with schizophrenia. Charlie was discharged.

Frightened of Everything

Charlie left the hospital even more suspicious of mental health professionals and institutions, and even less trusting of other people than he had been before. At the same time, I was beginning to understand some of the mysterious components of his disease, and the extreme threat his condition posed.

Now I wonder if long-term commitment might have saved him. If he'd been hospitalized for a year or so in an ideal place—a place I don't think exists, and if it did, insurance probably wouldn't cover— maybe he'd have been able to receive meaningful help.

Perhaps in such an environment, and with enough time, at least one doctor would have been able to form a rapport with Charlie, and find a mix of medicines that would have helped him. Maybe then Charlie could have found that help was possible.

As it was, our plans for Charlie to live in a halfway house after his discharge were short-lived. He fled after a day's stay.

He later sat at our dining room table and explained why he couldn't go back. "I've been going through a very difficult time," he told us. "And I'm frightened."

"What are you frightened of?" I asked.

"Everything."

So Charlie saw his psychiatrist, took his medication, and went for a few hours a week to a clubhouse for the mentally ill. We knew his heart wasn't in any of it, but we had been told, and had read, that although people with schizophrenia don't like structure, they need it.

Yet Charlie grew less and less engaged with the world around him. He had been a champion chess player, and loved all kinds of games, but each time I asked, he said he didn't want to play "right now." Except for endless bridge over Christmas week, when both his sisters were home, guaranteeing a constant foursome, he didn't play anything, with me or anyone else.

His father could often engage Charlie, for a little while, in conversations about sports, and I could sometimes do the same about flowers, those we saw and those I planned to grow, with him. But he was uninterested in our plans, and he didn't tell us about any plans he might have been making for himself.

Negative Symptoms

Charlie couldn't bring himself to go to class or get a job. He rarely watched television or read books, something he once did with a passion; the only thing he'd look at were the sports pages, and then only halfheartedly. Poor grooming accompanied his passivity, his sinking from the world. Nearly all his clothes were worn, and often torn and dirty, despite my offers to wash them and buy new ones. He didn't shower unless prodded.

Charlie had the negative symptoms of schizophrenia: lack of motivation and initiative, lack of interest in the world around him, an inability to plan, a loss of creativity. Negative symptoms can be subtle and difficult to interpret. It's not any one behavior, or even any combination of them, that necessarily leads to diagnosis. It's the damage they do, the way they make a person unable to lead a normal life, or to go on living any life at all, that demonstrate the disease.

Negative symptoms are hard, maybe impossible, to treat, despite claims made for the newest medications. Oddly (to those unfamiliar with the disease) people who suffer the positive symptoms of schizophrenia—talking to themselves, behaving inappropriately in public, hearing voices—generally have a better prognosis than those with negative symptoms. And a sudden onset of the disease suggests a better prognosis than a long gradual one like Charlie's.

The delusion Charlie harbored about death was especially threatening. Although he talked about it very little, we knew he held a belief that he could, through death, continue on earth but on a more interesting plane, one that involved time travel and mental telepathy and spaceships.

At Christmas time, he drew a childlike picture of a faceless figure, standing on an earth with no houses or other people. There are two tall trees and, high up in a gray sky, a spaceship. "Why do you want a spaceship, Charlie?" his twin sister asked. "Is it because you're sad?"

"No, doctor," he replied, but the mockery left his voice as he said, "I want a spaceship. I've wanted one for a long time."

Carrying Out a Long-Held Intention

One day, after several months at home, Charlie wasn't in his room when I went to tell him, as I did at 8:15 each morning, that I'd start cooking his eggs when I heard the shower stop. The police came right away. The search service of the National Alliance for the Mentally Ill helped look for him, too. I made call after call, some to strangers, hoping for a lead on Charlie's whereabouts.

Charlie had seen his psychiatrist, a skilled and experienced doctor, three days earlier, but the doctor hadn't perceived any imminent danger, nor had anyone else. Just the day before, Charlie had gone to the movies with friends; the only statement he'd made to them about his emotions was that he was bored.

As the days stretched into weeks, we all hoped Charlie was alive somewhere, off on an earthly adventure.

More than a month after he disappeared, a rower, out sculling on a Saturday morning, found Charlie's body. He had been in the river, the medical examiner said, a long time. The keys in his pocket were rusty, and his body, they told us, was unviewable. Ernie insisted on seeing him anyway. He looked like Charlie, he told me, but as if "he had been through a very hard time." We think he died the night he left home, carrying out a long-held intention.

The funeral was a big one, with many young people. The community in which Charlie had grown up grieved with us, as did people he'd met in college and old friends from all over.

Shortly after the funeral, a friend who hadn't known my son, but who has an all-too-intimate familiarity with mental illness, called. "I have nothing to say to console you," he said, "except this: You, and especially he, have been saved years and years of torment."

"Oh no," I said. "This is the worst thing that could happen."

If Charlie had lived, science and the social and medical system might have advanced enough to help him. His family and friends would have gone on trying. He might have found a path that would have allowed him to right the disorganization and disturbance of his mind enough to allow reconnection with life in a way that could grant him some peace, and even happiness.

Over the last decades, there has been progress in understanding and treating mentally ill people such as Charlie. Current thinking on schizophrenia holds that when Charlie was an embryo, some of the cells in his developing brain didn't migrate as they should have, and this biological error determined his disease—its timing and manifestation—from the outset.

Because the psychiatric community no longer blames families of sick people for their diseases, we are free to help our sons and daughters, brothers and sisters, mothers and fathers, instead of blaming ourselves. Medication helps many people, and more drugs are being developed all the time. We are coming to understand that every patient counts; it's a lesson taught us by creative advocates such as Moe Armstrong, who has tamed his own schizophrenia, and gone on to teach people with the disease to help each other. He is a model for what is possible.

Lamenting and Praying

I lament what was not possible for Charlie. I want him here. I want to sit next to him on the porch steps in the evening, and hear his voice. I want to see him smile again, however hesitantly. I want to be able to do one more thing for him, two more, a thousand more, a million. I want him back, sick or well.

For now, I do every sensible thing I can think of: make contributions to, and keep in touch with, the National Alliance for the Mentally Ill, live for the living, and commemorate Charlie in the way I conduct my own life. When I stand at Charlie's grave, I pray that as he died, his belief that he was going to a more interesting world was strong within him, so that he went in peace and expectation. I pray that he is free of fear, in a place full of goodness that he couldn't find in his short, far-reaching life.

I pray for all mentally ill people, and I pray that I can accomplish a lot, with humility.

I know now that what I said to my friend isn't true. Charlie's death isn't the most terrible thing that could have happened. To have been denied the grace of his life would be worse.

THE EFFECT OF SCHIZOPHRENIA ON SIBLINGS

Clea Simon

Clea Simon was raised in a home with two schizophrenic siblings. She explains that it took her years to realize that this experience had a lasting adverse impact on her emotional health and interpersonal relationships. Living in a home with a schizophrenic sibling can leave a child frightened, confused, and emotionally disconnected, Simon writes, and these traits often continue into adulthood. Siblings also live with the knowledge that they too have the genetic potential to become schizophrenic, according to Simon. A freelance journalist in Cambridge, Massachusetts, Simon is the author of *Mad House: Growing Up in the Shadow of Mentally Ill Siblings*, from which this selection was excerpted.

Katherine was screaming again. Her high, frantic wails had alerted the house almost thirty minutes before, and they continued in a constant barrage, each cut off only when she sobbed in breath. The bathroom walls seemed to tremble from the force of her voice as my father labored to remove the hinges of the door, and my mother, standing behind him, tried to pass some reassurance through the barrier, through the din. Katherine, my sixteen-year-old sister, had gone into the bathroom sometime in the past hour and had turned the simple lock for privacy. But then she had panicked, had somehow forgotten how to release the catch, and now she believed she was trapped. "It's OK, we're here. It's OK, we're here," my mother said, repeating the phrase like a mantra, trying to calm Katherine down. My father gave up on the hinges and began unscrewing the doorknob, taking it and the lock off to free my sister.

Although this scene is burnt into my memory, I have no clear recollection of where I was as Katherine's wails made that wood door vibrate. I must have been in the house to witness this. I was probably right across the hall, in my own bedroom, undoubtedly curled up with my nose in a book while the drama played out, in an attempt to avoid the pandemonium. Scenes like this had grown increasingly common as Katherine descended into schizophrenia. I was eight years old.

This was neither Katherine's last crisis, nor my family's only bout with mental illness. Not long after this scene, my brother, Daniel, then eighteen years old, would break down during his freshman year at Harvard and would be hospitalized, the first of many times. My beloved, normally outgoing brother had progressed from locking himself in his room for hours, with his music and his pot, to hearing voices. My brilliant brother could no longer differentiate between his mind's creations and reality.

By the time I was ten and moving from the *Black Stallion* books to *The Diary of Anne Frank,* both my siblings had been diagnosed with schizophrenia, with its delusions of persecution and bodiless voices telling of terrible things. By the time I was twelve and graduating to boy-girl parties, my brother and sister had been in and out of various institutions, hospitals, and halfway houses. Over the next few years, my siblings seemed so out of control, so potentially dangerous, that both were forbidden to return on any permanent basis to our family house in suburban Long Island. By the time I was fourteen, I lived as if I were an only child, growing up in a moderately affluent seventies suburb, and I let myself enjoy my solitary standing. Daniel and Katherine were out of the house, and I believed the problems that had come from living with them belonged to the past. I could not have been more wrong.

An Indelible Mark

As one does with an embarrassing memory, I avoided thought of my brother and sister and believed that since they had no role in my current life, they had no effect on my behavior. It would be another ten years before I realized that, far from having escaped my family's problems, I was buried in them. The illness that had taken control of my siblings' lives had made an indelible mark on my own, and denying the impact of their illness simply kept me from seeing, and countering, its effects. I wanted a life without mental illness, without the pain and confusion that my brother and sister unwittingly brought to me, and so I sought to leave them behind. But all my efforts at creating a new life scenario without my brother and sister, without their illness, sank me deeper into denial and despair.

In many ways, my family situation was not unique. Most of us grow up with some kind of dysfunction, as it is now known. Most of us carry it with us. We can do only what we know, and that for many of us means repeating the behaviors learned in our family, or reacting against them. I tried to break that pattern. For years after I left Long Island and my family home, I tried to pick up life as an adult by mimicking those around me, those who had what I saw as healthier families. It didn't work. I had poor luck with jobs and romances, but I couldn't see why. After all, I had functioned, and done very well, without much support during my early years. A smart, compliant,

COPING WITH MY SISTER'S SCHIZOPHRENIA

Pamela Gerhardt

Pamela Gerhardt describes the experience of watching her sister succumb to the symptoms of schizophrenia. She writes that her sister, who is extremely smart and creative, began to have frightening delusions and hallucinations and started to engage in a variety of dangerous behaviors. Gerhardt recounts her attempts to help her sister, who finally was involuntarily hospitalized and placed on medications that provided some relief. Although she is still on medication, Gerhardt's sister continues to struggle with symptoms, and Gerhardt remains concerned about her sister's well-being and worries that her own children may inherit the illness. Gerhardt is a freelance writer based in Washington, D.C.

On a spring day in 1994, my oldest sister called from St. Louis to tell me I was dead.

She spoke officially, as if she were a tour guide for the Pentagon. "When you were a baby," she explained, "Mom put you in a basket under the yellow sun and I watched you burn and melt. The earth cracked open and you fell in. When you emerged you were a replica of yourself. An impostor."

She would tell me this story again and again during that Easter season, several times a day, at 8 a.m., 11 p.m., 3 a.m. I was the one she always turned to. By the end of the week, I had purchased a plane ticket. I would fly to St. Louis and stand at her door and prove to her that I was, in fact, alive. She could pinch me if she wanted to. "See," I would say. "It's me."

Different

She had always been different. Now she was something else, something I could not name until I eventually filed an affidavit to have her involuntarily committed to the state mental hospital where she was diagnosed as a paranoid schizophrenic.

My sister, six years my senior and the oldest of five children, has passed along a lot of crooked information. All my life I have been lis-

Excerpted from "Hearing My Sister's Voices," by Pamela Gerhardt, *Washington Post,* August 2, 1998. Reprinted with permission from the author.

tening. Even now, even after the diagnosis, it is difficult at times for me to know with certain clarity what is truth and what is delusion. She was always the smart one. She won citywide art awards in high school. She taught herself to play, flawlessly, by ear, the piano solo from Eric Clapton's "Layla." She read Dickens, Tolstoy, the King James Bible, teaching me to follow suit. Before the illness, or perhaps as it was slowly unfolding, she taught herself German and Italian and how to sing opera. One Halloween, she dressed me up as Virna Lisi, and I proudly quoted my sister as I explained to my 16-year-old buddies that Lisi was "a late '60s B-movie screen goddess."

When we are young our older siblings tell us that thunder is the sound of angels bowling and we believe them. Such is the fabric of sibling trust.

Those of us who are close to the mentally ill want so much to believe that our loved one is simply different, perhaps even chosen, blessed. We struggle with the idea that we are somehow at fault, that we let things slip, that at some crucial moment we turned the other way. We must constantly rope ourselves in, remind ourselves that the illness is just that—an illness, impartial, arbitrary, and that it needs to be fixed.

"Touched"

Voices told Joan of Arc to go into battle, and St. Teresa of Avila had a vision that she was "pierced" by the love of God. Both women were sainted. Today, perhaps they would be institutionalized. Perhaps it is no mistake that in slang we say that crazy people are "touched." There is a certain wisdom and creative beauty in my sister's mental illness. Even her story of my death is eloquent, rich in detail, motion, color. It is that individual brilliance we sometimes glorify, hold on to in our mythology and popular culture: Think of James Stewart in *Harvey*; Dustin Hoffman in *Rain Man*; or the pianist David Helfgott whose story is dramatized in the movie *Shine*. It is the part we are most afraid to squelch with drugs or long hospitalizations. Often, hallucinations seem to be all that crazy people have to work with. Take away the dreams, we fear, and they go blank.

I come from a family of Catholic, rural European immigrants, and much of familial life seemed dense with the macabre, raw faith, premonitions. My grandfather's sister suffered from symptoms that I now believe were schizophrenia. At times, she destroyed things in her house with a hammer, convinced that they were evil. She would call mom at 3 a.m. to ask, "How is your mother?" seeming to forget at those odd hours that my grandmother had been dead a full 10 years.

Which immigrant brought the illness to America? I imagine schizophrenia as a forgotten acorn in a peasant's pocket, a memento from the Old World, carelessly overlooked by customs. And I've often wondered whether it would ever show up in my house, with my children.

My sister tells me that her doctor says this: "Maybe it is hereditary.

Maybe it is the Holy Ghost. The point is, to live with such hallucinations is more than any human can endure. Take your medication."

By now, many of us have come to learn, tragically, what can happen when a paranoid schizophrenic stops taking the medication. My sister recalls with shocking detail the horrible hallucinations and delusions that used to terrorize her: a nephew's head sitting on top of her VCR laughing at her and sticking out his tongue as she tried to watch the news; flying saucers on top of downtown buildings beaming green and purple cuss words into her brain as she passed by; a devil raping her. She calls me often to review the past, as if checking to see if it happened. She tells me she will never stop taking her medication.

Hospitalization

After my flight to St. Louis, my brother and I stood on her front porch. We knocked, but she didn't answer. I yelled, "Open up. It's me."

Finally, she cracked the door. "Who are you?" she asked.

She let us in after a few minutes. She showed me pictures, dozens of family photos I had seen many times. In every shot she had carefully, meticulously cut out my image. There was the family at Christmas with a hole where I should have been. She said she burned the pieces along with our grandmother's Bible, a handful of costume jewelry and a rotted fox stole in the back yard grill.

"You look like you," she said. My presence seemed to confuse her, puncturing her fiction.

We told her that we were going to the hospital and that we wanted her to come with us. We told her this many times. "Just a minute," she would say, then freeze as if listening. Finally, she would reply, in a different, raspy voice, "He says I don't have to go."

We left. We drove to the state mental hospital to sign affidavits, and on the way I realized she had not once asked what I was doing in St. Louis, how I had gotten there, where I was planning to stay. My brother parked his cherry-red Charger in a visitor space, and we both sat there a while and cried. St. Louis State hospital, now closed, was a spooky, Gothic building with tall, dark, barred windows that inspired many childhood stories. I had never once considered that someone I knew would have to go to a place like that.

Inside, as we wandered the halls looking for the right departmental office, we passed sealed doors with faded signs that said, "In Case of Elopement Ring Bell." Elopement. I had to think about that for a minute. Such a romantic word for the terror that must be associated with escape.

The hospital discharged my sister three weeks later with no plans for follow-up. The state can afford only so much. They handed her a bottle of pills, which she promptly threw in the trash. Confidentiality laws barred me from talking to her doctors. I had a week's worth of questions. Not one was answered.

During the next six months, she was arrested several times, once after a high-speed highway chase that ended with her car blowing up. She stole her neighbor's mail for a month. She threw her kitchen glasses at another neighbor's house. She called the chief of police of Rome more than 20 times one week to explain, in Italian, that the pope needed to be arrested. She poured a bottle of vodka into her car's gas tank. Finally, the police took her back to the hospital where she stayed for three months, received counseling, proper medication. I will always remember the day I sat in the chilly visitor's room and she said, finally, to my relief, "I have something called paranoid schizophrenia."

She knows I am writing this story. On the phone she presented me with a list of things to include: how no one would hire her as the illness progressed because her appearance and mannerisms began to change; how she was unemployed for five years; how the joblessness and low self-worth contributed to her madness; how she went through her savings; how the paint cracked off her one-bedroom, 100-year-old house; how the snow and rain forced a hole in the roof above her bathroom; how it took three years for us to get her on disability.

Today, on medication and living alone in her house in St. Louis, my sister no longer reads. She doesn't follow movies or the lives of stars. She doesn't cook, sing or play music or paint anymore. She stands too close to people. She rocks back and forth. She doesn't bathe very often. Mostly, she sits in her broken chair in the front room of her house and chain smokes and thinks about the past, the future, the state of the world, and then she writes it all down, sending letters to important people who never respond. She fixates on people, mostly men, who are clearly out of reach. She recently gave up on Piero Marini, the pope's master of ceremonies, after sending countless letters and notes. "I'm nobody," she said to me the other day, her words heavy with the realization that no one, ever, is going to take her to that place where the azaleas forever bloom. And every night when she tries to go to bed, small devils stand around her head and poke at her face, depriving her of sleep.

A day or so after the Capitol shootings [the July 1998 killing of two Capitol Hill police officers by a man with schizophrenia], my sister called, as she does whenever a paranoid schizophrenic makes the news. Always, she is upset, agitated, afraid. "Do you think I could kill someone?" she asks. Always, my answer is firm, simple. "Don't ever stop taking your medication."

We talk it out, and the conversation often ends with this: "He didn't know what he was doing," she says. "They have to understand."

She pleads with me, as if I can somehow call people up, shout from a mountaintop, make everything right.

Glossary

bipolar disorder Sometimes referred to as manic depression or manic-depressive illness; a disorder in which both **manic** and **major depressive** episodes are experienced in alternating phases.

delusion A false belief or incorrect inference about reality that is firmly sustained despite seemingly obvious evidence to the contrary. There are various types of delusions, including the following:

- **grandiose** A delusion of inflated worth, power, knowledge, or identity, such as believing oneself to be Jesus Christ.

- **persecutory** (or **paranoid**) Believing that one is being followed, spied on, harassed, attacked, or conspired against.

- **thought broadcasting** The belief that one's thoughts are being broadcast and can be perceived by others.

- **thought insertion** The belief that certain thoughts are being inserted into one's mind from an outside source.

hallucination A sensory perception that is perceived by one person but not by others. The most common hallucination experienced by persons with **schizophrenia** are auditory (sound), usually voices. Visual (sight) hallucinations also occur.

ideas of reference The thought that random external events have an unusual meaning that is specific to oneself. For example, persons with **schizophrenia** sometimes believe that events on television shows somehow refer to themselves.

major depressive disorder A disorder in which the patient experiences several symptoms of depression for at least a two-week period. Symptoms include persistent sadness, thoughts of death or suicide, loss of interest in activities formerly enjoyed, difficulty concentrating, weight gain or loss, inadequate or excessive sleep, decreased energy, and feelings of worthlessness, hopelessness, and guilt. Persons with major depressive disorder sometimes experience **psychotic** symptoms, such as auditory **hallucinations**.

mania A state of elevated, expansive mood, usually accompanied by a decreased need for sleep. Persons in a manic episode may experience irritability, euphoria, increased energy, racing thoughts, and **psychotic** symptoms, including grandiose **delusions**.

psychotic As broadly defined, refers to the **positive symptoms** of **schizophrenia**; also used more narrowly to describe **hallucinations** and **delusions** exclusively.

schizoaffective disorder A disorder in which one experiences the **positive symptoms** of **schizophrenia** as well as the symptoms of an affective (mood) disorder—most commonly **major depressive disorder** or **bipolar disorder**.

schizophrenia A severe mental illness that usually sets in during adolescence or early adulthood. Sufferers experience the following two types of symptoms:

- **positive symptoms** These include auditory or visual **hallucinations**, **delusions**, or disorganized speech and behavior.

- **negative symptoms** These include apathy, social withdrawal, and a lack of emotional expression.

ORGANIZATIONS TO CONTACT

The editors have compiled the following list of organizations concerned with the issues presented in this book. The descriptions are derived from materials provided by the organizations. All have publications or information available for interested readers. The list was compiled on the date of publication of the present volume; the information provided here may change. Be aware that many organizations take several weeks or longer to respond to inquiries, so allow as much time as possible.

American Psychiatric Association (APA)
1400 K St. NW, Washington, DC 20005
(888) 357-7924 • fax: (202) 682-6850
e-mail: apa@psych.org
website: www.psych.org

The American Psychiatric Association is a society of physicians who specialize in the diagnosis and treatment of mental and emotional illnesses and substance-use disorders. It helps create mental health policies, distributes information about psychiatry, and promotes psychiatric research and education. The APA publishes issue briefs, fact sheets, the pamphlet *Schizophrenia*, and the monthly *American Journal of Psychiatry*.

American Psychological Association (APA)
750 First St. NE, Washington, DC 20002-4242
(202) 336-5500 • fax: (202) 336-5633
e-mail: psycinfo@apa.org
website: www.apa.org

The American Psychological Association is the primary professional organization of psychologists. Its aim is to "advance psychology as a science and profession and as a means of promoting human welfare." The APA produces many publications, including the monthly journal *American Psychologist*, the monthly newspaper *APA Monitor*, and the quarterly *Journal of Abnormal Psychology*.

Bazelon Center for Mental Health Law
1101 15th St. NW, Suite 1212, Washington, DC 20005-5002
(202) 467-5730 • fax: (202) 223-0409
e-mail: bazelon@tidalwave.net
website: www.bazelon.org

The Bazelon Center provides technical and legal assistance in selected court cases involving mental health law. It also advocates for increased consumer (patient) participation in the design and operation of mental health services. The center publishes handbooks, manuals, issue papers, and reports on key legal and policy issues related to mental health, including the issue of involuntary commitment.

Canadian Mental Health Association (CMHA)
2160 Yonge St., 3rd Fl., Toronto, Ontario M4S 2Z3 CANADA
(416) 484-7750 • fax: (416) 484-4617
e-mail: cmhanat@interlog.com
website: www.cmha.ca

The CMHA is a voluntary organization that seeks to promote mental health and serve mental health consumers. The association conducts research, workshops, and seminars on mental illness, runs housing and employment programs, and engages in political advocacy to improve Canada's mental health system. It offers numerous publications, including the pamphlets "Mental Health for Life," "The Myths of Mental Illness," and "Schizophrenia."

Center for Psychiatric Rehabilitation
Boston University, 940 Commonwealth Ave. West, Boston, MA 02215
(617) 353-3549 • fax: (617) 353-7700
e-mail: kaos@bu.edu
website: www.bu.edu/sarpsych

The center is a research, training, and service organization that seeks to better the lives of persons who have psychiatric disabilities by improving the programs and systems that serve them. It adheres to the principles of psychosocial rehabilitation, primarily the belief that persons with psychiatric disabilities have the same goals and dreams as any other individual: a decent place to live, suitable work, social activities, and friends to turn to in times of crisis. The center publishes the *Psychiatric Rehabilitation Journal* four times a year.

National Alliance for the Mentally Ill (NAMI)
Colonial Place Three, 2107 Wilson Blvd., Suite 300, Arlington, VA 22201-3042
(703) 524-7600 • fax: (703) 524-9094
website: www.nami.org

NAMI is the nation's largest self-help and family advocacy organization solely dedicated to improving the lives of people with severe mental illnesses, including schizophrenia. It works to decrease stigma and advocates for improved treatment and insurance coverage for people with mental illnesses. NAMI offers numerous policy papers, fact sheets, and brochures to the public, as well as the monthly newsletter *NAMI Advocate* and books such as *Breakthroughs in Antipsychotic Medications: A Guide for Consumers, Families, and Clinicians.*

National Empowerment Center (NEC)
599 Canal St., Lawrence, MA 01840
(800) 769-3728 • fax: (978) 694-9117
e-mail: necwest@earthlink.net
website: www.Power2u.org

The NEC is an organization run by current and former mental health patients. Its goal is to promote the philosophy that people who have been diagnosed with mental illnesses can recover and take charge of their own lives. The center publishes the *NEC Newsletter* and posts many newsletter articles on its website, including "People Can Recover from Mental Illness" and "Hearing Voices That Are Distressing: Self-Help Resources and Strategies."

National Institute of Mental Health (NIMH)
6001 Executive Blvd., Room 8184, MSC 9663, Bethesda, MD 20892-9663
(301) 443-4513 • fax: (301) 443-4279
e-mail: nimhinfo@nih.gov
website: www.nimh.nih.gov

The NIMH is a government agency that seeks to improve the treatment and prevention of mental illness through research in neuroscience, behavioral science, and genetics. It publishes fact sheets and booklets on schizophrenia. The Surgeon General's landmark report on mental health is available on its website.

National Mental Health Association (NMHA)

1021 Prince St., Alexandria, VA 22314-2971
(703) 684-7722 • fax (703) 684-5968
e-mail: infoctr@nmha.org
website: www.nmha.org

The association strives to promote mental health and prevent mental disorders through advocacy, education, research, and service. The NMHA publishes fact sheets, position statements, and pamphlets on schizophrenia and mental health policy, including the pamphlet *Schizophrenia: What You Should Know.*

National Mental Health Consumers' Self-Help Clearinghouse

1211 Chestnut St., Suite 1207, Philadelphia, PA 19107
(215) 751-1810 • fax: (215) 636-6312
e-mail: info@mhselfhelp.org
website: www.mhselfhelp.org

The clearinghouse provides information and technical assistance to the consumers' movement, a group of past and present consumers of mental health services (sometimes referred to as "survivors" or "ex-patients") who strive to improve the mental health system and help one another recover from mental illness. Its publications include background papers and political alerts on policy issues as well as the newsletter *The Key.*

Treatment Advocacy Center (TAC)

3300 N. Fairfax Dr., Suite 220, Arlington, VA 22201
(703) 294-6001 • fax: (703) 294-6010
e-mail: Info@psychlaws.org
website: www.psychlaws.org

The center is dedicated to reforming local, state, and national laws to make it easier to provide involuntary treatment to persons with severe mental illnesses such as schizophrenia. The center's founder, E. Fuller Torrey, is a renowned advocate of increased treatment for the mentally ill. His articles, including the briefing papers "The Effects of Involuntary Medication on Individuals with Schizophrenia and Manic-Depressive Illness" and "Violence and Severe Mental Illness," are available on the center's website. TAC also produces numerous fact sheets and briefing papers.

BIBLIOGRAPHY

Books

Nancy C. Andreason, ed.
Schizophrenia: From Mind to Molecule. Washington, DC: American Psychiatric Press, 1994.

Patricia Backlar
The Family Face of Schizophrenia: Practical Counsel from America's Leading Experts. New York: G.P. Putnam's Sons, 1994.

Michael Ferriter
Schizophrenia and Parenting. Aldershot, England: Ashgate, 1999.

Sheldon Gelman
Medicating Schizophrenia: A History. New Brunswick, NJ: Rutgers University Press, 1999.

Tara Elgin Holley
My Mother's Keeper: A Daughter's Memoir of Growing Up in the Shadow of Schizophrenia. New York: W. Morrow, 1997.

Gwen Howe
Working with Schizophrenia: A Needs Based Approach. London: Jessica Kingsley, 1995.

Nathaniel Lachenmeyer
The Outsider: A Journey into My Father's Struggle with Madness. New York: Broadway, 2000.

Peter E. Nathan, Jack M. Gorman, and Neil J. Salkind
Treating Mental Disorders: A Guide to What Works. New York: Oxford University Press, 1999.

Jay Neugeboren
Imagining Robert: My Brother, Madness, and Survival. New York: W. Morrow, 1997.

Joel Paris
Nature and Nurture in Psychiatry: A Predisposition-Stress Model of Mental Disorders. Washington, DC: American Psychiatric Press, 1999.

Ming T. Tsuang and Stephen V. Faraone
Schizophrenia: The Facts. New York: Oxford University Press, 1997.

U.S. Department of Health and Human Services
Mental Health: A Report of the Surgeon General. Rockville, MD: U.S. Department of Health and Human Services, 1999.

Sophia Vinogradov, ed.
Treating Schizophrenia. San Francisco: Jossey-Bass, 1995.

Peter Wyden
Conquering Schizophrenia: A Father, His Son, and a Medical Breakthrough. New York: Knopf, 1998.

Periodicals

Sharon Begley
"Lights of Madness," *Newsweek*, November 20, 1995.

Thomas J. Billitteri
"Mental Health Policy," *CQ Researcher*, September 12, 1997. Available from 1414 22nd St. NW, Washington, DC 20037.

Susan Brink
"For Severe Mental Illness, a Higher Profile and New Hope," *U.S. News & World Report*, December 20, 1999.

Fox Butterfield | "Prisons Replace Hospitals for the Nation's Mentally Ill," *New York Times*, March 5, 1998.

Fox Butterfield | "Treatment Can Be Illusion for Violent Mentally Ill," *New York Times*, July 28, 1998.

Judy Foreman | "Clues but No Answers on Schizophrenia," *Boston Globe*, June 21, 1999. Available from P.O. Box 2378, Boston, MA 02107.

John Gibeaut | "Who Knows Best?" *ABA Journal*, January 2000. Available from 750 N. Lake Shore Dr., Chicago, IL 60611.

Erica Goode | "Doctors Try a Bold Move Against Schizophrenia," *New York Times*, December 7, 1999.

Erica Goode | "With Help, Climbing Back from Schizophrenia's Isolations," *New York Times*, January 30, 1999.

Wray Herbert and Rachel K. Sobel | "Fearsome Madness," *U.S. News & World Report*, August 10, 1998.

Issues and Controversies On File | "Mental Health Policy," February 4, 2000. Available from Facts On File News Services, 11 Penn Plaza, New York, NY 10001-2006.

Daniel Judiscak | "Why Are the Mentally Ill in Jail?" *American Jails*, November/December 1995. Available from 2053 Day Rd., Suite 100, Hagerstown, MD 21740.

Joseph P. Kahn | "A Schizophrenic's Tale," *Boston Globe*, June 1, 1995.

Julie Marquis | "Erasing the Line Between Mental and Physical Ills," *Los Angeles Times*, October 15, 1996. Available from 202 W. First St., Los Angeles, CA 90012.

Julie Marquis | "No More Shame," *Los Angeles Times*, June 3, 1997.

Mark Nichols | "Improved Treatments Ease a Cruel Disease," *Maclean's*, January 30, 1995.

Susan Okie | "A Viral Source for Schizophrenia?" *Washington Post*, November 9, 1999. Available from 1150 15th St. NW, Washington, DC 20071.

Sean Paige | "The Devil in Deinstitutionalizing," *Insight on the News*, September 14, 1998. Available from P.O. Box 91022, Washington, DC 20090-1022.

Sally L. Satel | "Real Help for the Mentally Ill," *New York Times*, January 7, 1999.

Jolie Solomon | "Breaking the Silence," *Newsweek*, May 20, 1996.

Elyse Tanouye | "New Weapons in the War on Schizophrenia," *Wall Street Journal*, August 25, 1999.

E. Fuller Torrey | "How Did So Many Mentally Ill Persons Get into America's Jails and Prisons?" *American Jails*, November/December 1999.

E. Fuller Torrey

"Let's Stop Being Nutty About the Mentally Ill," *City Journal*, Summer 1997. Available from the Manhattan Institute, 52 Vanderbilt Ave., 2nd Fl., New York, NY 10017.

E. Fuller Torrey and Mary T. Zdanowicz

"We've Tried Mandatory Treatment—and It Works," *City Journal*, Summer 1999.

E. Fuller Torrey and Mary T. Zdanowicz

"Why Deinstitutionalization Turned Deadly," *Wall Street Journal*, August 4, 1998.

Traci Watson

"Quieting the Voices," *U.S. News & World Report*, October 28, 1996.

Barbara Wickens

"Unwell and Untreated: The Mentally Ill Are Having to Cope on Their Own," *Maclean's*, August 10, 1998.

James Willwerth

"Working Their Way Back," *Time*, November 22, 1999.

INDEX